# Seven Figure Trading

Written By:

# Robert Savoy

Publisher: Success For Life
Cover Design: Bridgett Cavanaugh
Production and Composition: Amy Messina-Genova

Copyright © 2020 by Success For Life
All rights reserved.
Reproduction or translation of any part of this work beyond that permitted by Section 107 or 108 of the 1976 United States Copyright Act without permission of the copyright owner is unlawful. Requests for permission or further information should be addressed to the Administrative Department of Success For Life.

This publication is designed to provide accurate and authoritative information in regard to the subject matter covered. It is sold with the understanding that the publisher and author are not engaged in rendering legal, accounting or other professional services. If legal advice or other expert assistance is required, the services of a competent professional should be sought.

Library of Congress Cataloging-in-Publication Data
    Savoy, Robert M. 1970—
    [Seven Figure Trading]
    Seven Figure Trading / by Robert Savoy
    p. cm.
ISBN-10: 1-7336267-3-6 (alk. paper)
ISBN-13: 978-1-7336267-3-6 (alk. Paper)
1. New York Stock Exchange. 2. Speculation. I. Title

Printed in the United States of America.

# www.SevenFigureTrading.com

> Beneath the broad tides of human history there flow the stealthy undercurrents of the secret societies, which frequently determine in the depth the changes that take place upon the surface.
>
> — A. E. Waite —

**LEGAL DISCLAIMER AS REQUIRED BY LAW: There is a substantial risk of loss trading the stock market with or without this or any other advertised product, service, or system. Past results are not necessarily indicatives of future results. No representation is being made that any account will or is likely to achieve profits or losses similar to those shown.** Except where identified as actual profits, references to profits may reflect profits in hypothetical or simulated trading. Hypothetical or simulated performance results have certain inherent limitations. Unlike an actual performance record, simulated performance results do not represent actual trading. Also, since the trades have not actually been executed, the results may have under- or over-compensated for the impact, if any, of certain market factors, such as lack of liquidity. Hypothetical trading results are also subject to the fact that they are designed with the benefit of hindsight. No representation is being made that any account will or is likely to achieve profits or losses similar to those shown. Be aware that investment in any of these markets including stocks, bonds, options, futures and/or ETFs have large potential rewards, but also large risks. You must be aware of these risks and be willing to accept them to invest in the markets. Do NOT trade with money you can't afford to lose. Your decision to trade any market – whether presented as low risk or high risk – should be based on your particular financial circumstances and trading objectives. You can achieve profits far less or far greater than represented in these materials. There are absolutely no income guarantees. **Always trade at your own risk.**

# Table of Contents

| | |
|---|---|
| Introduction: How the "Trading Bug" Bit Me | 7 |
| Chapter One: How I Met Dr. Peter Barrington | 13 |
| Chapter Two: What to Trade, What <u>NOT</u> to Trade | 17 |
| Chapter Three: The Backstory of *The Master* of Trading | 28 |
| Chapter Four: Market "Tricks" That Never Work | 35 |
| Chapter Five: An Overview of How to Use *The Slice* | 38 |
| Chapter Six: Which Markets to Look At Trading | 45 |
| Chapter Seven: The Three Main Market Indicators | 52 |
| Chapter Eight: Getting Started Trading | 61 |
| Secret Society Member Reveals Shocking Admission | 68 |
| Secrets of the Wall Street Maverick | 77 |
| Testimonials | 115 |
| Frequently Asked Questions (FAQ) | 116 |
| Statement from Geoffrey Gold | 120 |
| Auto Mechanic Profits $74,262 in His First 63 Days! | 121 |
| More Testimonials | 122 |
| Legal Disclaimer | 124 |

This Book is Dedicated to My Wife Charlene and My Son Christian…

*Everything I Do, I Do It For You*

## Introduction
## How the "Trading Bug" Bit Me

When I first got introduced to the concept of trading for a living, I was in college. I knew this kid – well, I guess he wasn't really a "kid" by definition – but he was a dude in my college dorm right across the hall. He looked all of 12 years old but he was the same age as the rest of us. And since I can't remember his name right off the top of my head, I remember we called him The Wiz Kid for the reasons I'm about to explain.

I went to ULCA film school because I had this idea that I was going to become the next Martin Scorsese or Oliver Stone. So, I moved across the country from Boston in 1988 at the ripe age of 18 with wild visions of grandeur in my eyes about how I was going to strike it rich in the movie business as the next hot shot Hollywood director. All I remember wanting to be my whole entire life is a film director. Little did I know that life had other plans for me.

So, back to The Wiz Kid. He was getting a degree in screenwriting. And if I recall correctly, he wasn't very good at it either. I remember him bringing some of his script pages over to me one night for an opinion since he knew I was striving to be a director. I gave him the most positive review of his crappy work as possible since it wasn't my place to squash his dream but I knew he just didn't have that "it" factor to be successful as a Hollywood writer. I could tell right away.

Apparently, I didn't have that "it" factor to be the next big shot Hollywood director either because I never did fare well in the industry. I was never able to get further than getting an internship as a screenplay reader at a B-rate studio called Cannon (later 21$^{st}$ Century). You know, the company that did the old subpar Charles Bronson and Chuck Norris films? That was the company I worked for. Remember, it was an internship so I never really "worked" for them in the sense that I actually got paid. But what I did learn from that position was that most people don't know how to write scripts worth a damn and the grind of the Hollywood business (as I saw it) really sucked. It wasn't all the glitz and glamour that I thought it would be.

But my college days weren't a complete waste of time, even if I wasn't able to follow my dream to become a rich and famous Hollywood director. The Wiz Kid turned me on to something that would begin to change my life forever.

I had a job in college at a local deli making sandwiches and salads during the week and as a bartender on the weekends to pay for college. My parents paid a little money for school but I was mostly on my own. What I noticed is that The Wiz Kid didn't have a job. He didn't get a full-ride scholarship either. So, one day, I had to ask him how he was able to pay for school, pay for dates with chicks, and pay for his brand-new 1989 black Corvette Z51 he got that year. All without a job and a trust fund from as far as I could tell.

I had to find out. Remembering that his less-than-stellar screenplay was a talking-heads *Wall Street* trading flick, I told him I wanted to chat with him about a movie idea I had and that maybe he could write the screenplay for my better-than *Wall Street* movie idea which was the hit film just a short time before that. He was so excited that he could hardly resist.

When I got there with a case of beer and a notepad, he was none the wiser about my true intent on being there. My goal was to pump him for as much information as possible about how he was able to make money while sitting on his ass while the rest of us sweat at menial jobs, taking up hoards of time, while struggling to keep up our bare-minimum required GPA to stay in school.

At first we started talking about my *Wall Street* meets *The Godfather* script idea but I think The Wiz Kid quickly figured out that my story idea wasn't well-thought-out at all as he anticipated; I could see his disappointment as his overall demeaner went from excited to a deflated sadness. He didn't like my story's logline of, "A bankrupt mob boss decides to scam Wall Street out of millions by getting insider information by blackmailing publicly traded company corporate executives." I know, it was a pretty dumb story idea. But at least it got me in the door with The Wiz Kid.

"It needs a lot of work," he said.

"Yeah, I know. That's why we're sitting here, right? To work out the story details?"

"I mean, it's not bad. I guess. It just needs work."

"So, what do you think about the premise of the story?" I asked.

"The mob boss obviously knows nothing about Wall Street," he said.

"How so?"

"Your logline…it's just not *believable*? Anybody who knows anything about trading on Wall Street knows…it's just not believable."

"What do *you* know about trading on Wall Street?" I asked.

He didn't answer for the longest time. Then he suddenly got up from his squeaky office chair and went over to his corner desk area. He slid a small book off his makeshift "bookshelf" on his desk.

"My dad gave this to me before I came here. He's an investment banker. But he didn't give me a dime to go to school because he thought I should earn my way through school like he did. But he did give me this book and told me that if I wanted to make money like he did, all I had to do was read this little book." He held it in his hands, not wanting to give it to me and not wanting me to touch this seemingly "holy" little book he was holding.

"So, what's the book? What's it about?" I was very curious at this point. I wanted to look at the book but he didn't let me see it and he didn't pass it to me so I could look. He just held it in his hot little hands. "Can I see it?"

"No. This is a really old book that my dad gave me to read and I'd rather not say where he told me he got it. He told me to keep this to myself."

"Okay, so what's this magical book about then? You must want to tell me otherwise you wouldn't have gone to the trouble to go over to your desk to get it." I was getting the idea that he was regretting telling me about this book because now he opened himself up to the possibility of me stealing it, not that I'd ever do that. But I could tell that this thought was clicking inside his head as I could read the sense of immediate regret on his face.

"I can tell you a little bit about this but…you have to promise to never tell anyone about what I'm going to tell you."

And I've never mentioned anything about The Wiz Kid or his secret book. I'm still not going to tell you where his dad got the book, what the name of the book was, or exactly what the contents of the book was because a promise is a promise.

But I will tell you this one thing:

It was about a unique way of looking at the stock market with specific financial instruments to trade them in a way where one who trades using those techniques could potentially be profitable a whopping 90% of the time.

What was strange about my encounter with The Wiz Kid is that he gave me some very basic information over about an hour and then he told me that he'd prefer that I knew no more than what he told me. He abruptly ended our conversation and he then told me to leave. No wonder this guy never had any friends. He had the social aptitude of an aardvark.

After that encounter, he purposely avoided me, avoided eye contact, slammed doors quickly as I passed his room, dodged me through hallways and around corners. I guess he was afraid I'd stop him and say something like, "Hey, can you tell me more about that book of yours?" Or even worse (for him), to break into his dorm room and steal the book.

He only lasted a year at UCLA and then he left. I don't know if he dropped out of school or transferred elsewhere. And since I don't remember his real name, I can't look him up to see what ever happened to him. He's probably one of those behind-the-scenes wizzes of Wall Street. Who knows? But since that day, I never stopped thinking about that little book he had, what secrets it held, and how he was able to make so much money trading stocks with the secrets he knew. I could never find a copy of that book but I'm still looking for it in every old bookstore I venture into.

## *Chapter One*
## How I Met Dr. Peter Barrington

Fast forward to 2011 when I attended a Monica Main apartment building real estate investing event in Atlanta, Georgia. I happened to be sitting at a group dinner table with an older man by the name of Dr. Peter Barrington the first evening of the event. I politely asked the man what he hoped to gain from the event and he said, "Well, I made a lot of money trading the markets and I want to learn how to invest that money in commercial real estate. How about you? What do you do?"

"I'm in sales." Yes, that's right. I ended up dropping out of UCLA after my second year and never ended up being that hot shot movie director I had hoped to become. Instead I went back to Boston with my tail between my legs, having been chewed up and spit out by the proverbial Hollywood devil and got a job for a large car dealership and never turned back.

"Sales. I love sales. It's one of the only working careers where you can make whatever you want to make," Dr. Barrington said.

"What do you mean by 'working careers'"?

"Just what I said. Sales is a working career. You make money when you work but sales allows you to have a much better leverage on your time versus what you make at an hourly-wage job…no matter how hard you work, you still make a set hourly wage. But if you work harder in sales then you have the opportunity to make more money."

I had to ask. "So, stock trading is a 'working career,' isn't it?"

"No. It's not. It's investing. It's not a job or a career. Totally different," he said.

"Do you teach people how to do this stuff?"

"Unfortunately, I don't. This is something I learned when I was a kid and I don't have any plans on telling people what I do or how I do it. Sorry."

And the conversation just kind of died after that. Was there anybody out there who could teach me how to successfully trade stocks?

After that event, I decided to start buying a bunch books on trading stocks. I delved into those books harder than I ever did in my years as a college student. I figured that these secrets to trading stocks had to be somewhere in those books. The problem was…how was I ever to know which book had the secrets and which were just junk?

The answer: the hard way. That's how. I took some of my commission checks from my car sales and opened my first margin account. I started using the techniques in different books to place trades. Long story short, I lost over $60,000 trying each and every strategy in every one of those books. I tried trading stocks, bonds, ETFs, commodity futures, options…anything you can think of, I tried to trade.

So, I gave up. And I'll be honest with you. And I never planned on trading anything ever again.

Then 2018 rolled around. I had a really rough year prior to that. I ended up divorcing my wife of 22 years in 2017 and I had lost my dad in the same year to cancer. It was really a rough year for me.

At the same time, I felt my sales career was beginning to unravel. I had worked my way up to a finance manager and was making pretty good money. But I hated every second of my new job position. Yes, I was making more money than being on the floor as a regular Joe Chump car sales guy but I felt like my life was diminished to selling tire and paint protection plans all day to people who probably didn't need or want either.

When I was going through my personal life disasters in 2017, I was just dialing in work and my superiors were beginning to notice. I think the job position shift was an attempt to see if they could get me back on track as being the super sales guy I used to be. Instead, I felt like they shoved me into a tiny box where I'd end up dying in that small office doing needless upsells and car registration paperwork to cranky customers who had been in the showroom for way too long trying to get rebates and discounts.

Life just stopped making sense to me. What made the least sense is that I'd have to do something for a living that I hated more than anything just to pay my bills. There had to be another way. There had to be a way for me to live a better life.

But…what did that look like? I had to find out one way or another.

# Discover How You Can Grab the Highly-Coveted Rules of Trading Checklist You'll Refer to Again and Again Throughout Your Profitable Trading Journey…For FREE!

## To Discover How You Can Obtain These POWERFUL TRADING RESOURCES That You'll Be Using to Direct Your Most Profitable Trades FOR FREE…Call Our 24-Hour <u>HOTLINE</u> Now at:

# 1-800-990-0028

CALL 24 HOURS A DAY!

## *Chapter Two*
## What to Trade, What <u>NOT</u> to Trade

In early 2019 *The Slice Trading System* was released for the first time. Admittedly, I thought it was just a gimmick…until I saw Dr. Peter Barrington's name on the brochure. Then I knew it was real. This was the *same guy* I had a conversation with 8 years before. I was so excited about *The Slice*, I was beside myself!

But I was sad at the same time. Dr. Barrington was dying. And this was the only reason why he felt it was time to share his secret trading system: *The Slice*.

I ordered it right away and dived squarely into it. I locked myself in my bedroom on a long weekend and consumed every morsel of that system from front to back, top to bottom, and side to side. I went through it with highlighters, ink pens (for notes in the margins), sticky flags, and a notebook for more in-depth notes. At first I was taken aback by how much information was in the system but as I went through it a third time, it all "clicked" into place for me, especially when I watched the special training video on exactly how *The Slice* works.

Since starting to trade using *The Slice* technique, I've been very successful using it and I'd like to share my levels of success with you and how I've become so successful using this secret.

I think the most difficult part for me has been trying to erase all the bad stuff out of my brain that I had learned over the years about trading. I found myself constantly comparing *The Slice* to other trading methods and it quickly messed me up. Sometimes I'd try to add *The Slice* to other techniques or combine several strategies together. This is a huge no-no and even Dr. Barrington warns against this.

Let's try to start with a blank slate from here on out. Forget *everything* you know about trading.

As you know, the stock market itself is full of publicly traded companies. How it works is this: When a company is said to "go public" through an IPO or "initial public offering," they do this usually with the intent on raising capital for expansion. Investment banks will underwrite the shares after it's been determined how many shares and at what price they will be offered. These banks will become the owners of these shares and will then sell them to the public with the idea of selling them for more than what they bought them for…obviously to make a profit. So, the stock market is made up of thousands of publicly traded companies like Amazon, Disney, 3M, Microsoft and Apple, for example.

With the publicly traded companies I mentioned, there are larger markets that host kind of a "basket" of some of the most powerful, profitable, and stabilized companies. These "baskets" are the

S&P 500, for example, where there are 500 companies in this basket. The NASDAQ is another one with over 3,000 companies, unless you're talking about the NASDAQ 100. There's the Russell 2000 which has 2,000 small-cap companies in it. This is what we call the stock index markets or the *stock indices*.

You can't really trade the S&P 500 directly. Like there is no S&P 500 stock for you to trade because it's an index market. But you can trade a futures contract or option for the S&P 500. Your other option is that you can trade an ETF or exchange-traded fund that tracks the S&P 500. All the rest of these stock indices pretty much work in the same way.

I don't trade commodities or futures…which are the *same thing*. Dr. Barrington used to trade S&P and NASDAQ futures contracts back in the day before the ETF alternatives were available. Once the ETFs came out, he stopped trading futures altogether because they are extremely volatile and there is *tremendous risk in commodity trading*.

Of course, it's up to you if you want to apply any trading method you learn – whether from here or from somewhere else – to trading futures but it's not recommended you do this. Maybe you want to use *The Slice* on NASDAQ or S&P futuress. But Dr. Barrington does *not* trade futures anymore. I don't trade futures. And this *The Slice System* isn't about trading futures so if you decide to use what you learn here to trade futures, it's your funeral.

**We recommend trading exchange-traded funds or ETFs.**

You are probably wondering: *Why does he seem so adamantly against commodity futures trading?* There's a really good reason for this: with futures contracts – which is the only other way you can trade a "basket" market like the S&P 500 or the NASDAQ – you MUST be right with your position, whether you're long or short. If you're not 100% right, when the market moves against you – even just a tiny bit – you not only find yourself in a losing position, watching your margin account drain out by the minute, but you don't have the luxury of waiting around for the market to correct itself and to move in the direction you want it to go into because you'll either be stopped out or you'll get a margin call. And that *just sucks*.

With a commodity futures contract, you are only putting in a "down payment" or a small percentage of the total contract, something like 5 or 10% of the total value of the futures contract. So, say it's 10%. This means that you are leveraged 10 to 1. And if the market moves against you – which usually it does for a time in any position in the market – you are wiped out pretty quickly. And you lose everything you have really fast. Faster than you may think. It's a *very* dangerous position to be in.

An alternative – to *lessen* risk – might be to trade something called the e-mini market like the mini-S&P 500. These are smaller contracts. But, again, the risk and volatility are still there, just on a much smaller basis. So, why go down that path at all?! I wouldn't do that. It's just not worth it. You shouldn't take that kind of risk either. It's pointless and completely unnecessary.

So, why ETFs then? Why not individually publicly-traded companies? Why not just use *The Slice* for, say, trading Amazon stocks, for example? Because there are too many things that go wrong with trading on an individually publicly traded company. Even though stock trading is <u>supposed</u> to be based on the concept of supply and demand, many times it is not. Company scandal, for instance, can drive the value of a stock *down* even if the actual company itself is relatively financially robust. While supply and demand is *supposed* to be the parameter of the ups and downs of the value of a stock, we all know that there are many, <u>many</u> other factors that have almost nothing to do with the fiscal value – good or bad – of a company. That's just a dangerous way to trade.

In all fairness to stable companies like Amazon, Microsoft, 3M, and Disney, for example, it's probably a much better strategy to look at these more like a long term buy-and-hold kind of deal rather than as a day trading opportunity, for instance. If you are fairly sure that Disney will be around forever and they'll keep getting bigger and bigger – as in their fleet of ever-expanding Disney ships for the Disney cruise line, not to mention their time-share sales and house-building endeavors – can't you see how socking away Disney shares on the long haul would be more of a retirement kind of strategy…and not really short term at all? At least that's the smart way to look at it. Disney – and the companies like Disney – have to be looked at as kind of a buy-it-and-keep-it type of stock trade. That's where the money is made in those kinds of stocks, not in day trading. Not in turn-around trading or short-term holds. It's in the long term where the value is.

      This is why so many people get this wrong and why almost everybody loses money in stock trading; they look at it in a completely wrong light on how to do this. They look at it as some kind of get-rich-quick deal and they usually end up jumping into the get-poor-quick boat instead simply because they don't understand the proper trading function of these stock instruments.

      Now, since the type of trading that I'm going to show you is for short-term trading, this is why we're not looking at long-term stock positions like we'd consider with solid and robust publicly traded companies like the big boys I was referring to before. For short-term trading and for the kinds of profits that you are probably interested in – and because we're not talking about messing with the high risk of futures trading – there's an alternative to all of it, to be able to trade short-term to be able to make the kinds of money that you're aiming for, whatever that may be, as everybody has different goals. But, let me just tell you, the sky is the limit with the strategy that I'm about to show you.

Let's continue covering the basics. So far, we've gone through why we're not touching individual stocks for the purposes of short-term trading. Later on, after you make a stockpile of money, you should strongly consider laying some of that money into long-term stock trades with solid and robust companies like Disney but as a long-term retirement nest-egg kind of strategy. In other words, you'll be dumping the money into the stocks with the intent on basically buying the stock and forgetting about them for as long as possible. That's a really good strategy and should be used to diversify your portfolio.

But back to the subject at hand: short-term trading. How can you make money with much shorter trades? Remember, I'm not here to show you here how to wait decades to make money. And I'm sure that's not why you're here either.

**Commodity futures are off the table due to the high risk and volatility. Remember that.**

We talked only briefly about the alternative: *exchange-traded funds*…or ETFs, for short.

But how are these any better. After all, aren't these more like boring mutual funds with more of a jazzed-up name to them?

They are kind of like mutual funds but they are traded more like a stock. And they're profitable as all hell because, if you trade these correctly, you can – in many cases – mitigate a huge amount of risk while sweeping in the profits from being on the right side of the market. Now, don't get me wrong. *There is risk in <u>everything</u>.* There is risk in rolling out of bed and driving to work. There is risk in eating in a restaurant. There's risk when you hop on that airplane to your next vacation in Bora Bora. *There is risk in absolutely everything.* So, when I say that the risk is mitigated…it's to a certain degree. No risk is completely abolished. That's just not possible. I mean, even sitting in your living room can have some degree of risk. You never know. A jet plane could crash into your house, somebody can shoot you through the window, or a meteor could crash through your roof. The likelihood that any of these things is probably slim but it's all still a possibility, even if it's remote. So, I do have to tell you that. *There is risk in trading the markets.*

If you were to trade an S&P 500 futures contract, for example: that would be equivalent to walking across a swamp full of very hungry alligators on a tight rope on a windy day…and after about 2 hours of tight-rope-walking training. That's what THAT is like.

Trading an ETF that tracks the S&P 500 like the iShares Core S&P 500 ETF (IVV): that would be equivalent to walking across that same swamp of hungry alligators on a tight rope but there is a thick piece of glass or a sturdy net that is 6 inches below your rope and the 'gators are underneath. So, if you fall, you have a chance of survival. Of course, things could go wrong with this too. The glass or net could break. But I hope you get my point. It's a much different scenario.

Nobody is _completely_ safe. But you can do things – trade certain markets, for example – to help to really mitigate any potential loss in trading while allowing you to make profits like a madman or madwoman. And the first step in mitigating that loss is by making the right choice in what markets to trade. So, ETFs is the way to go for that.

There are a lot of ETFs to trade. My favorites are the QQQ and the SPY markets. But I've done really well with all kinds of ETFs like the SPDR (pronounced "Spider") Gold Trust, the iShares 20+ Year Treasury Bond ETF, and the Vanguard Small Cap ETF, just to name a few. But there are A LOT of ETF markets I've traded and made a lot of money from.

Is there any ONE market that is "better" than the other? Not really. It all comes down to personal preference. Like me, you'll find 2 or 3 markets that are your favorites because you'll get a handle on their unique personalities. Yes, markets have personalities. And the faster you can figure out the personality of 2 or 3 markets, the more money you can make. Seriously, that's what it boils down to at the end of the day. Understanding market personalities and applying The Slice to it.

*The Slice* works really well on ETFs and I recommend you take different charts for different ETF markets just to get a feel for how they work, how The Slice plays out on the charts, and which you have a good vibe about. I know that's not a scientific or mathematical way to make a decision – by getting a "vibe" about a market – but why not? Right? It works for me. It works for most traders I know. Ever trader I know has market preferences – or markets they like to trade – and when you ask them to drill down into why they like certain markets, their answer is nothing more than just having a feel for specific markets. They like how they move. They seem more in-tuned with certain markets. And it's kind of unexplainable. The only way you'll get there is by working with the markets, looking at charts, and practicing on paper before you trade in the real markets. And I'll show you as best as I can in how to work through all of this.

The second step to all this is by learning a consistent and reliable strategy to help you map out forecasts of your trades. That's a big deal, obviously. And that's where *The Slice* comes in. This is the strategy you've been waiting to hear about, waiting to learn, and chomping at the bit to use to help you make successful trades. I'm going to tell you a little bit about *The Slice* and how it works.

## Did You Call For Your Free Jesse Livermore Action Checklist Poster and Free Audio Seminar Yet?

## If Not, GET IT NOW!

**Discover How You Can Grab the Highly-Coveted Rules of Trading Checklist You'll Refer to Again and Again Throughout Your Profitable Trading Journey...For FREE!**

To Discover How You Can Obtain These POWERFUL TRADING RESOURCES That You'll Be Using to Direct Your Most Profitable Trades FOR FREE...
Call Our 24-Hour <u>HOTLINE</u> Now at:

# 1-800-990-0028
*CALL 24 HOURS A DAY!*

## *Chapter Three*
## The Backstory of *The Master* of Trading

To start off, I'd like to tell you a little bit of backstory leading up to this and a little bit about Dr. Barrington's story about how he came to know *The Slice*. I should mention this trading secret wasn't actually called *The Slice* when it was used by both Jesse Livermore and Bobby B., Dr. Barrington's granddad who taught him how to use this strategy. If I'm not mistaken, it was Bobby B. who began referring it to *The Slice* because he felt he had to call it something. Up until that point, it was kind of a nameless technique that none of the big traders talked about but they all used it. It was so secretive that it never had a name until Dr. Barrington's grandfather learned about this technique and he felt that he had to call it *something*. So, he was the one who named it *The Slice* for clarity, I'm guessing. I don't know for sure.

I'm getting a little ahead of myself here. Sorry. I'm just really excited to be telling you all of this because this is powerful stuff!

Dr. Barrington grandfather's name was Robert Barrington (AKA "Bobby B."). Bobby B. was friendly with a man by the name of Jesse Livermore. You may or may not have heard the name "Jesse Livermore" before. (I'll tell you more about who Jesse is in a minute.) Dr. Barrington's grandfather and Jesse were pretty close friends. During the times they spent together, Jesse would share things with Bobby B. about how to trade

the markets the REAL way (rather than the way Livermore wrote about in his books).

Now you're probably wondering...*who the hell is Jesse Livermore?*

*Jesse Livermore was the only one (on record) to predict the stock market crash of 1929 to the day it happened! And he warned people of this upcoming market crash for months before it happened!*

So, Jesse Livermore is one of those guys who not only had a knack in accurately forecasting the markets to the day of impending changes but he shared his trading secret with only one person in the whole world: Bobby B. Dr. Peter Barrington's grandfather.

The details about how Bobby B. and Jesse Livermore is a little sordid. Both men were drunks and womanizers. I guess that's the story that isn't so popular but it's the truth so I have to mention it here. Bobby B. and Jesse Livermore started their friendship while scoping out the scene for new women to have affairs with while hanging out drinking together for the purposes of hooking up with women. This would be during the 1920s and the 1930s. They became fast friends during this time frame with the common interest of hanging out, getting drunk, and scoring with women even though both were married men.

While Jesse Livermore *never wrote* about his secret trading method behind how he scored $100 million by shorting the stock market on Black Tuesday (October 29, 1929 stock market crash) that set off the Great Depression, he <u>DID</u> tell Bobby B. how he did it, *in precise detail during the years they hung out and partied together!*

Most people falsely assume that Jesse used a trading strategy called *The Shakeout + 3* but that's NOT how he knew that the market was going to crash nor is it how he was able to accurately forecast the market pivots long before everyone else knew what was happening. If you take a look at this double-bottom pattern, it's designed to forecast an upcoming bull market, <u>NOT</u> a bear market at all.

Plus, as Jesse himself said, *any fool* can recognize the *Shakeout +3* pattern.

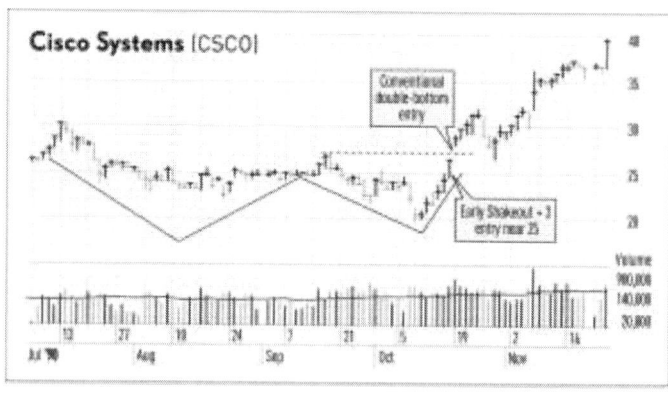

Here's how it works: A cup-with-handle buy point *(10 cents above the high of the handle)* or a flat-base buy point *(10 cents above the high of the left side of the base)*. The conventional buy point comes when the stock starts to rally after the second leg down. Then entry is when the stock crosses above the middle peak in between the two down legs. Add 10 cents and there's your buy point.

*The Shakeout + 3* pattern also comes when a stock starts to rally after the second leg has formed. The buy point is derived by adding three points to the low of the first pullback. So, if the low was 27, add 3 points to get a correct entry at 30. However, the adding of 3 points generally only applies to stocks that are trading in the 20-40 range and require strong volume when a stock clears the proper buy point.

With higher-priced stocks, it's critical to add more than just 3 points to the first low. It's best to add around 10% of the price of the stock, in this case. If the stock is priced at 60, you can add 5 or 6 points to the low to get the buy point. For stocks that are trading at 100 or more, add 8 to 10 points. This "double-bottom pattern" was in Jesse's book called *How to Trade in Stocks*. It was one of the very rare things Livermore discussed in his writings about any "secret trading method" he might have used to when predicting major market moves.

But it's *not really* how he traded, especially when predicting huge market crashes

"Bobby B" Barrington and a young Peter Barrington at the Age of 12

(which is how *big money* is made very quickly). There was actually a completely different way he forecasted and accurately predicted the market…a way that he NEVER wrote about or revealed *to anyone else* <u>except</u> to Dr. Barrington's grandfather!

Dr. Barrington remembers when his grandfather would talk *incessantly* about trading stocks and *The Slice* method that Jesse Livermore had shared with him *many times* over the years… which was the *real* trading method he had used for the hundreds of millions of dollars he had made in the stock market. His grandfather even drew out illustrations of "The Slice" and showed him how it can work when trading almost anything. But the young Peter Barrington never cared. He was just a young kid. Who would care about stock trading at only 12 years old? I know I wouldn't!

Back then, Peter would mow his grandparent's acre-and-a-half of lawn every week. He'd give the young Peter a "bonus" by adding an extra 50 cents on top of the regular buck he'd normally earn from mowing the lawn *if* he could draw *The Slice* on whatever stock chart his grandfather chose for that week.

Of course, young Peter would do it. He'd earn an extra 50 cents just from drawing a few lines on a piece of paper which took him maybe 25 seconds on his slowest day. Bobby B. would always smile then would give young Peter 6 quarters, and then he'd walk away with the stock chart Peter had drawn on.

Little did young Peter know what his grandfather was *actually trading* with what he'd had marked on those drawn-on charts until 6 years later when…

**Bobby B. Showed Young Peter a Margin Account That Had Over $100,000 in It…And Told Him It Was HIS MONEY from HIS Stock Predictions**

**All from a Starting Margin Account of Only $500; And <u>Here</u> Is How It Was Done…With Jesse Livermore's SECRET Trading Strategy Called…**

## *The Slice*

If you've ever had experience with stock, option or bond trading before, these names would probably be familiar to you. They've all written books: Warren Buffett, W.D. Gann, Larry Williams, Ted Warren, Peter Lynch…Yet, why does it seem that no matter how many trading techniques, strategies, and secrets investors waded through most NEVER find the true trader's "secret" to fortunes?

*After all, the key to success in the markets is to know ahead of time what the market will do. That is how REAL traders make a fortune like clockwork.*

*But REAL traders who make REAL money will NEVER give you a secret investing strategy that actually works. Why? Because the bottom line is this:*

**REAL Traders Know a Trading "Prediction" System That <u>GUARANTEES</u> Successful Trades At Least 90% of the Time But They <u>CANNOT</u> Reveal Their Secrets to You!**

Many traders will use geometrical patterns to predict the market. William Gann was famous for using these patterns, although some have said that he wasn't that successful at trading. He was successful at selling books and courses about trading but wasn't really successful using the strategies he taught people. Or so some people have said. None of us know the truth. But Gann was big on the geometric patterns on charts. He was even known to use astrology to forecast market shifts and changes!

---

**If You Didn't Call Yet, NOW IS THE TIME! Discover How You Can Grab the Highly-Coveted Rules of Trading Checklist You'll Refer to Again and Again Throughout Your Profitable Trading Journey...For FREE!**

**To Discover How You Can Obtain These POWERFUL TRADING RESOURCES That You'll Be Using to Direct Your Most Profitable Trades FOR FREE...
Call Our 24-Hour HOTLINE Now at:**

**1-800-990-0028**

CALL 24 HOURS A DAY!

## Chapter Four
## Market "Tricks" That Never Work

Several traders I know (including myself) have used geometric patterns to help them forecast the market so the concept itself isn't new at all. This has been going on for decades as a tool for forecasting the markets. Nothing new there at all.

But…what is different is this one particular geometric pattern called *The Slice* because it's pretty unique in and of itself.

So, when I first got into this, right away I started to wonder how I'd be able to use *The Slice* on charts in our high-tech world. I mean, does anybody really draw patterns on a paper chart anymore? I'm a Gen Xer. Everything is on the computer. Everything is online. So, how does this work…drawing patterns on paper? I mean…really? Is this still a thing?

And I quickly found out that, not only is it still a thing, it's the preferred thing. Like most people in the world of trading, I bought into two different very expensive and very popular stock trading software programs. One was just over $5,000. The other was just under $10,000. One of the software programs – the more expensive one – required hands-on training for in an office for about three days. I had to fly out to the west coast to get the training. I was able to figure the software out. It wasn't that hard. The problem was that I had lost money using *both* of the software programs when it came time to applying those "forecasts" to real trades using real money. What a disappointment that was!

Sometimes certain software is okay if all you want to make is a couple hundred bucks a day...and that is before you usually have to give it all back in losses. But if you want to make some real money, those programs really don't do squat for you...at least they didn't for me at all. I doubt they really work for most people because otherwise you would have heard it all over the news and in every investment magazine and newspaper about how earth-shattering and great it is...but you never hear about software for the most part...from anybody for that matter. So, it's a false path and bad thinking that a computer can and should do all the work for you while you laze around watching TV all day. That's really not the way to go if you want to really do well using *The Slice*.

I did hear that they were working on a computer software program for *The Slice* but I don't know when that will be ready to go. It would be great if something like that did come out soon but I'm okay with printing out charts and drawing my patterns on a sheet of paper with a pencil, a ruler, and a compass when needed. Yes, it's pretty old-fashioned but it works like a charm!

You don't need expensive software or fancy online mapping gadgets to attempt to tell you where the market will go. All you need is your brain, a pencil, a piece of paper, and *The Slice* technique That's all you need to be successful in doing this. And if you're too lazy to print out a chart to do the work by taking a pencil to paper then you're definitely *not* cut out for this. So, plan on keeping your day job instead, I guess, and keep watching those reruns of *Friends* and *Seinfield*.

But if you're willing to follow protocol in working *The Slice*, then you have the potential of being very successful with this trading secret.

# Check Out *The Slice* Video RIGHT Now!
# www.TheSliceVideo.com

**Ready to Get Started with The Slice? Give Us a Call at (661) 295-5050 Ext. 2 and Talk to a Trading Expert Who Can Better Help You Understand How The Slice Can Potentially Change Your Financial Future!**

## *Chapter Five*
## An Overview of How to Use *The Slice*

As a starting point, one of my favorite ways of getting a chart online is through *Yahoo! Finance*, **TradingView.com** or **BarChart.com**. All of these are free charting services. If you're not sure how to find it online, just go to Google then type in Yahoo! Finance or type in TradingView.com or BarChart.com. You'll get right to the link for these sites.

In *Yahoo! Finance*, for example, at the top of the *Yahoo! Finance* website, there is a search bar that allows you to put in the stock symbol that you want to take a look at. You'll also notice that all the majors – the S&P 500, the Dow, the NASDAQ, and the Russell 2000 are all at the top. These, among others, are going to be the markets that you'll be tracking so that you can trade the ETFs that track these markets.

Yes, you'll be trading the ETFs that track the top stock index markets like the S&P 500, the Dow, the NASDAQ and others. But, let's not get ahead of ourselves here. When first "feeling out" a market that you may want to trade, you'll go to the "horse's mouth" first or directly to the stock index you are looking at tracking. (You don't go to the ETF first. You always go to the stock index and its charts first before doing anything else.)

Yes, we want to trade the ETFs that track these major stock index markets. But we need to *first* begin our research with the stock index we want to track. I like the S&P 500 a lot. I've made a lot of money with the S&P 500 as I have with the NASDAQ. Both of these stock indices are my "solids," I call them. This means they are my "go to" markets for the ETFs I trade. So, I generally will mostly trade the ETFs that track these two (2) stock index markets.

Because we are tracking these indices, it makes sense to look at the index market charts *first* when doing your charting and forecasting work. Yes, you will ALWAYS look at the index market charts FIRST before looking at the ETF market you are going to actually trade.

So, for example, if you want to trade an ETF that tracks the S&P 500 called the SPY market, you'll FIRST look at the actual S&P 500 charts FIRST and then you will look at the ETFs that track these markets *later on*.

If you are using *Yahoo! Finance*, you'll look at the top of the page and then you'll click at the top on the S&P 500 link. You'll see something called a "Summary." This, for the most part, is kind of useless because we need to get into the nitty-gritty of what's actually happening in order to begin our charting work. You will need to click on the "Chart" link that's just to the right of the "Summary" link.

When doing this, you will immediately get to something called an "Interactive Chart." This allows you to do a bunch of stuff on the chart if you want. The problem is, they don't have anything called *The Slice*. They have other things you can apply to their chart but not *The Slice*. And that's okay. I'm going to tell you how you're going to create your own "Interactive Chart" kind of the old-fashioned way.

As a first timer looking at the market for the very first time, it can seem kind of intimidating because you really don't know what you're looking at or where to start. It can seem overwhelming, like you're looking at a bunch of gibberish or something.

I remember my grandfather struggling to trade the markets and he'd look at a bunch of really small numbers listed in the newspaper every day. That seemed crazy to me. Now, with the super tiny numbers in the back of a newspaper, I still don't know how to follow all that. It makes no sense to me at all. I have to look at a chart because that's how I've trained my brain with this process through Dr. Barrington's training. You're going to be trained the same way; you'll be looking at charts and not a pile of numbers. The kind of charting service or platform you decide you want to use will be up to you. But I can make some suggestions for you.

Let's talk about your first chart, the very first one you'll want to look at and print out. It's called a "Historic" chart. These charts will go back decades and it gives you a really good idea of where the market is *right now* in comparison to where it's been in decades past. After all, how are you ever to know whether the market is now trading low, medium, or high in comparison to years or decades before if you don't look at the overall scope of things? You can't. It's just not possible.

For a clearer and non-distracted view of a historic chart, you may want to click on the "Bar" version so you don't have to see green and red colors. This will give you the most basic view of the chart which is what we want. You will see that the historic chart for the S&P 500 goes back to about 1950. When you use your mouse, you can pull back to the longest view. But you can zoom in if you don't want to see as many years. I like to see everything that I'm dealing with right off the bat. In this case, I can see the S&P 500 trading down at around 17 back in 1950. In comparison, I can see it trading as high as 2900 but most recently around 2700. Big difference from the last century, obviously.

Another thing I look at is the highest it was to date. So, the low was in the very early 50s at 17. By the late 60s, according to the historic chart, was when it was trading around 108. This is a big difference in only 18 years. Then in the 1990s, it was trading around 1000. To date it's almost triple that price! This market will just keep going up and up, probably forever.

As a quick recap, you want to find the stock index that you're going to be trading on with a tracked ETF for that market. Use *Yahoo! Finance* unless you have another chart preference somewhere else. Then take a look at the "Historic Chart" for this market to get an idea of where the market is trading now in comparison to years and decades past. Under the charting view pull-down options, I like using "Bar" for the purposes of this historic view. For some reason, looking at black on a white chart is easiest for me, but it may be different for you. You might want to choose another option like a "Colored Bar," for example. There's no right and wrong way to look at this historic chart. It's just for comparative reference of how the market was trading then in comparison to how it's trading today.

Please note: For really long historic charts dating back several decades, you'll have to pan over to the right by clicking the right arrow to get the rest of the history on the chart. For the S&P 500, it goes back to 1950 on this historic chart so it cuts off after 1968. You'll have to pan to the right to be able to see the years of trading after that.

As a side note, I recommend you get yourself a 3-ring binder. Again, this is doing it the old-fashioned way that, as a Gen Xer, I would normally be totally against because I'm a computer addict. But I've personally the power of being hands on in this process by simply printing out charts and drawing directly on them with a pencil, just the way

Dr. Barrington always does it. And since it worked very well for him, I'm in no position to argue with big success like that. And because he trains charting by doing it this way, I've learned this way. I've had some incredible trading successes by doing it this way so I recommend you follow in Dr. Barrington's footsteps by doing it the right way. Your trading success is in the balance so you don't want to take short-cuts otherwise you risk not forecasting the markets the right way and likely you'll lose money on your trades by being lazy. So, print out your charts, draw on them with pencil, and do it the right way. You'll be surprised at what you see on the charts by doing it this way and what you'll usually miss by *not* doing it this way.

When you print your charts out, you'll want to put them in your 3-ring binder with any notes you write or geometric patterns draw on them. It's much easier to reference physical copies of these charts rather than going back online each time you want to look at them.

One important tip I wanted to mention here: they've done studies that have suggested that the things we read or look at on a screen of any kind including laptops, computer monitors, smart phones, tablets, and even on the Kindle doesn't commit to memory the same way as when you're looking at a physical copy of something. I don't remember where I read about the study or the specifics of it, probably because I read it online somewhere and, as I just said, we don't remember as much of the things we've seen on any kind of screen. Kind of ironic, isn't it? Since the study I read about was online, I can't remember exactly what the study was about but I do remember that we don't retain as much information when we see it or read it on a screen.

With my own personal experience with this, I can attribute this as a fact for myself. I remember close to nothing I see or read online. I remember everything I read if it's in a magazine, book, or a newspaper.

**Did You Call For Your Free Jesse Livermore Action Checklist Poster and Free Audio Seminar Yet?**

**Discover How You Can Grab the Highly-Coveted Rules of Trading Checklist You'll Refer to Again and Again Throughout Your Profitable Trading Journey...For FREE!**

**To Discover How You Can Obtain These POWERFUL TRADING RESOURCES That You'll Be Using to Direct Your Most Profitable Trades FOR FREE...
Call Our 24-Hour HOTLINE Now at:**

**1-800-990-0028**

## Chapter Six
## Which Markets to Look At Trading

Let's talk about the markets you are aiming to trade. Let's start with the most notable of all which are the S&P 500, the NASDAQ, the Dow Jones, and the Russell 2000. This is just a starting point. You can go for more stock index markets or stick with the ones I mentioned. You can even narrow it down to one if you'd like. There's plenty of money to be made in one stock index and one ETF to trade that one stock index market, believe it or not. There are many others stock indices that I haven't listed but these are the ones I generally like to focus on. And as I mentioned before, my 2 favorite ETF markets are the SPY and QQQ which track the S&P 500 and NASDAQ.

If you choose to track a whole bunch of stock indices, you'll end up being confused and you won't have the laser-focus needed for ultra-accurate trades. Instead of diversifying – like probably been told to do – FOCUS ON ONE OR TWO MARKETS.

I don't care how proficient you think you are. We're all human and realistically we can focus really well on 1 or 2 things. When you're throwing 5 or 10 different things in the mix, it doesn't matter how focused you think you are, you can't do really well with that many markets at one time. Nobody can focus really well on 5 or 10 things with precision and accuracy. And you don't make money by throwing a bunch of spaghetti at the wall to see what sticks. You get rich by focusing like a laser beam on the select few markets that you jive with. Make sense? I hope so. Okay, so let's get into this.

I usually focus on the S&P 500 market and maybe you'll want to start there too. That's up to you. Aside from the historic chart – which is something you'll use as to reference to see where the market has traded and is trading now – there are 3 key charts that you'll be referring to all the time: a monthly, weekly, and daily chart. For me personally, I don't focus so much on the daily chart. I'm not a day trader and I find that it's a waste of time to focus on it.

I am in the business of *swing trading* and therefore we look at charts that service forecasts in that way. A swing trade, in case you don't know, is staying in a trade for days, weeks, or even months. Therefore, those are the charts I'll focus most of my attention on.

I personally tend to hold my trades for anywhere from a couple of weeks to about a month, maybe a bit longer. I definitely don't consider myself a day trader, so I don't really focus a lot on the dailies. I focus much more on the weekly and monthly charts, cutting it down to 2 focal points. I focus a lot on the 1-year chart, then the 6-month and 3-month charts when preparing to forecast a market using geometric patterns and angles. Remember, the more you simplify this, the more money you can potentially make. The more you make this complicated, the more money you'll likely end up losing. Try not to make this more complicated than it needs to be.

When using the *Yahoo! Finance* charts, I want to get you into the habit of changing your view into a bar or colored bar. It's up to you on which you prefer the most. First, take a quick look at MAX by clicking on the MAX tab at the top of the page just to refresh your memory on where we are trading in comparison to years past. We're trading high and according to the chart, we only traded higher than where we are now in February 2020. This nugget of information will come in handy a little later on as you begin to line up your market forecast before placing a trade.

Your next step is to print out this chart. Ideally the chart will fit the entire piece of paper if you can get it to print that way. I will usually hit the PRINT SCREEN key on my keyboard then I will paste it into a blank landscape Word document with that is in landscape with very narrow margins. After I copy the chart using the PRINT SCREEN key, I'll go into the Word document and right-click to paste it into my blank landscape narrow-margin document. Then I'll pull the corner with my mouse to make the chart part in the middle as big as possible, sometimes even going more narrow with the margin setting. Then I'll print it. This is pretty fast for me and how I got used to doing this. You can do it any way you'd like if you have a better printing system.

Another way of doing this is to use BarChart.com, find your market, and click on FULL SCREEN. Then click on MAX to get a MAX chart. Their charts don't go back as much as the ones you find on Yahoo! Finance but that's okay because once you make your assessment on where we are trading (in comparison to decades past), you can use a different service to print a chart. It's easy to use BarChart.com because all you do is click on the three (3) horizontal lines to the right of where it says "tutorial" at the top of the chart and the second to the last option says "Save Chart as Image (.png)." When you click on this, it will start downloading automatically into your Download file on your computer. You can then copy the file into a Word or Publisher document to make sure it maximizes your full sheet of paper then press print.

The good news about printing out these historic charts for a specific market is that you only have to do it once in a blue moon. You're not going to be printing these MAX or historic charts every week because they don't change much from one week to the next due to its length of duration and information it provides. You may not be printing 20-year, 10-year or 5-year charts that often either. So, once you print these out and put them in your 3-

ring binder, you won't have to keep doing the same printing work over and over again because these charts will be good for a little while at least.

After checking out the historic or MAX chart view, I want you to take a look at the 10-year and 5-year chart. Again, you'll also want to print this one out and you'll definitely find it to be easier doing this through BarChart.com.

All of these print-outs will be drawn on, notes will be jotted down on them, and they'll go into your 3-ring binder. This is really important because if you think you're going to miraculously remember all of your work, charting, and research, think again. You'll be looking at so many markets and nobody has a memory like that, unless you have a photographic memory. Even still, print, draw, write notes, and keep it all in a binder, preferably with tabs for each main market type like the S&P 500, the Dow, the NASDAQ, Russell 2000 for example. I went to Staples and got myself a package of 5 tabs for the following markets: S&P 500, Dow Jones Industrial Average (DJIA), the NASDAQ, the Russell 2000, and the Nikkei 225. I could have gotten 8 tabs but I wanted to narrow my trading decisions down to these markets. I ended up only focusing on the first three and ditched out the Russell 2000 and Nikkei 225. However, in the very beginning, you're not going to know which market "personality" you most have an affinity for until you look at all the charts, see which ones seem to interest you the most (based on their movement), and which you will settle on practicing trading first. Remember, you'll start by trading ONE market and not a whole bunch at the same time. This is a disaster in the making if you plan on recklessly trading a ton of markets at once in the beginning. By doing this, you'll likely end up being on the losing side of every one of your trades due to a lack of focus. So, if you remember nothing else I tell you in this book, remember this one thing: **FOCUS ON TRADING <u>ONE</u> MARKET ONLY TO START!**

The next chart you'll look want to print out will be the 2-year chart. Now, I know earlier I said that you'd be looking at a 1-year chart but I've found that to get a better perspective of 1 year of trading, it's much easier for me to see what's going on when clicking on the 2-year chart. It's actually quite a different prospective when comparing a 1-year and 2-year chart side-by-side. Otherwise the perspective is way too close when only looking at the 1-year chart. When I start getting the perspective of things happening in the market, I'll narrow my view down to the 2-year chart. Later I'll start delving into a 1-year, 6-month, 3-month, and 1-month chart. But, we need to first stop at the 2-year chart to get our initial patterning perspective.

Overall, the key 2 charts I focus on for longer-term trades is this 2-year chart and a 6-month chart, which I'll get to in a minute. Yes, you can drill down with a 1-year, 3-month, 1-month or 5-day chart if you want but that's not really going to give you the right perspective you need to do your charting correctly. It's recommended that you look at EVERY chart to make sure you get every kind of possible market perspective before making your trade because you may have missed something critical!

Right now you're probably thinking: what am I looking at? Good question. And now is not the time to start feeling overwhelmed or confused because we barely got started here.

**Did You Call For Your Free Jesse Livermore Action Checklist Poster and Free Audio Seminar Yet?**

**Discover How You Can Grab the Highly-Coveted Rules of Trading Checklist You'll Refer to Again and Again Throughout Your Profitable Trading Journey...For FREE!**

**To Discover How You Can Obtain These POWERFUL TRADING RESOURCES That You'll Be Using to Direct Your Most Profitable Trades FOR FREE...
Call Our 24-Hour HOTLINE Now at:**

**1-800-990-0028**

*Call 24 Hours a Day, 7 Days a Week!*

## *Chapter Seven*
## The Three Main Market Indicators

There are three (3) main market indicators when it comes to forecasting the market. I'm going to start with the easiest and most obvious first. It's called the ALL-TIME LOW OR HIGH pattern. This is self-explanatory. This is when the market is either trading at an all-time low or all-time high, as I talked about before. It doesn't take a genius to figure out where we are based on looking at that very first chart I told you about: the historic (MAX) and then the 20-year chart.

For the S&P 500, the all-time low was in 1950 when it was trading just under 17. The all-time high was in February 2020 when it was trading just over 3400.

What I like to do is come off the historic chart and do a shorter version to see where we stand, including the past 20 years. Looking back on the last 20 years, the lowest was in March 2009 at just below 650. Wow, was that low! By the way, these markets do directly reflect what's going on in the economy. Obviously when these kinds of markets are trading high, we're doing well. When they drop or they start performing poorly, we're struggling as an economy. That's just the reality in how these markets work.

So, in recent years (after the 2008 market crash), at one point in March 2009 we were trading below 650 but we have been on an upward trend (for the most part) since that time. So, in our most recent history, this would be considered our recent low. Again, this becomes important when we hit these market lows and highs because it becomes a completely no-brainer in what the market will do next. It's simple. When the market is low, it bounces back up. When it's really high, there's a big drop that will happen (as we're expecting to happen in the near future). And where we are now, it looks like we're coming off the high from early 2020 which means that at some point there will have to be market "give" considering that – at NO point in history, the market has NEVER just gone up forever without falling down – a market drop is in the future somewhere. This gives us the gist of the trajectory of the market, by letting us know which way the market is pulling. Up or down. And in this case, based on our quick all-time-low and all-time-high analysis, we can tell that we hit an all-time high in early 2020 (and even now) which means the market will begin pulling down for the next couple of years, at least. Possibly longer.

    This is also an indicator that we're moving into a market recession. So, that's another thing to prepare for in other aspects of your life if, for example, you want to sell your house and move somewhere else. In some leading markets it's probably already too late to sell but, again, since we're slipping into another recession and you can tell by looking at charts like these, it allows you to prepare in other areas of your life too.

The next market indicator are your support and resistance lines. Here's what it looks like on a 6-month chart from BarChart.com for the S&P 500:

You can also work with the support and resistance lines on a 3-month chart which may make better sense to you. Here's what it looks like:

Drawing these lines is more of an art than a hard science. We're mostly concerned with drawing the lines from most current market movement rather than lining them up directly with any movement that happened earlier (or in the left portion of the chart). This is why you'll notice some line overlap on the left side of the two charts on the previous pate. It's because we're mostly concerned with drawing the support and resistance in line with what's happening most recently (or the activity on the right of the chart) than perfectly lining it up with what happened before that (on the left side of the chart).

The final indicator that we use (before getting to *The Slice*, which is the MAIN market indicator), is the median line. This can only be drawn in AFTER the support and resistance lines are added to your printed charts. Taking the 6-month chart from the bottom of the previous page, here's how the median line would look after putting in the support and resistance lines:

The median (sometimes called "medium" line) is the dotted line above. What does this mean?

This line indicates kind of a "middle ground" for the where the market is trading. There's another way to get this "middle ground" number. Depending on the type of chart you're using (1-year, 6-month, or 3-month chart), you can take the highest number, the lowest number, add them together and then divide by 2.

So, for the 6-month chart on the previous page, the lowest number (price) traded in this time frame is 2,924. The highest number is 3,340. (We round up or down to the nearest tenth.) We add both together to get 6,264 then we divide by 2 to get 3,132. That is our median point or number. So, you don't actually have to draw this median point. You can just calculate to get the correct median number.

What does all this mean? This is our starting point before we can begin to draw in *The Slice* to make our final market forecast.

But…remember, we're not actually trading the stock index market directly because we're not going to trade a futures contract to be able to trade, for example, the S&P 500 or any of the stock indices. So, our next step before finding The Slice and planning our trade is to focus on the ETF that tracks our stock index. In this case, we'll be looking for a market that tracks the S&P 500. I like trading the SPY but there are others you can choose from such as the iShares Core S&P 500 ETF (IVV) and Vanguard S&P 500 ETF (VOO).

Now that we've done our basic charting work on the stock index itself (in this case, the S&P 500) we can now look at the charts for our selected ETF that tracks the S&P 500. For all intents and purposes here, I'll be selecting the SPY ETF market (that tracks the S&P 500) because it's my favorite market to trade.

Since we've already printed out all of the S&P 500 charts for our 3-ring binder, it's now time to delve into the SPY charts. This is a critical step because we won't know where the pricing is of the market we're trading without looking at the exact market we'll be placing trades for. Yes, the pricing is way off. The S&P 500 might be trading at 3,390 today but the SPY market may be trading at 337. As you can see, both of those price points are completely different even though the trading trajectory (up and down) is exactly the same with both markets.

When we say that these ETFs "track" a specific market (in this case, the S&P 500), it means it goes up and down precisely as the market it tracks does. It's just that the price points are completely different as I pointed out above. Since we're not trading the stock index market directly (because we're not trading commodity futures contracts), we need to now focus on our selected ETF that is tracking this market. Remember, each ETF that tracks the S&P 500 (or any other stock index) will have different pricing. The SPY may be at 337. At the same time the VOO may be at 310 and the IVV may be at 339. All at the exact same time. Yet they all move in precise unison (up and down) with the S&P 500 because they are all ETFs that track that market.

Since I'm focusing on the SPY market, I'll be typing in SPY at the top of BarChart.com, for example. This way I can download these SPY charts in the same order that I did for the S&P 500. What was that order again?

1) Historic (MAX)
2) 20-Year
3) 10-Year

4) 5-Year
5) 3-Year
6) 2-Year
7) 1-Year
8) 9-Month
9) 6-Month
10) 3-Month
11) 1-Month
12) 5-Day
13) 1-Day

Yes, that's a lot of charts. In the beginning, you'll want to download and print them all out. However, later on, you'll want to take a "short cut" by just downloading the CRITICAL charts which are your 20-year, 5-year, 2-year, 1-year, 6-month, 3-month and 1-month charts. (To get the closest trading view you'll need, you'll also download a 5-day chart, usually *right before* placing your trade to be certain of where the market trajectory is going.)

Just like what we did with the stock index market charts, you'll be doing the same thing with your key three (3) market indicators:

1) All-time low/high
2) Support and resistance
3) Median line

Once you get this down on your charts, you'll then have one more step which is to find *The*

*Slice. The Slice* is the last component you'll need when lining up your trade that you'll be placing online. (Long gone are the days of calling a broker on the phone. It's all online now.)

## Did You Call For Your Free Jesse Livermore Action Checklist Poster and Free Audio Seminar Yet?

## If Not, GET IT NOW!

**Discover How You Can Grab the Highly-Coveted Rules of Trading Checklist You'll Refer to Again and Again Throughout Your Profitable Trading Journey...For FREE!**

**To Discover How You Can Obtain These POWERFUL TRADING RESOURCES That You'll Be Using to Direct Your Most Profitable Trades FOR FREE... Call Our 24-Hour HOTLINE Now at:**

# 1-800-990-0028

## Chapter Eight
## Getting Started Trading

There are several brokerage houses you can use to trade from such as Ameritrade.com, Schwab.com, or eTrade.com to name a few. I personally use Ameritrade.com and I believe Dr. Barrington does too, if I'm not mistaken.

The minimum amount to start a margin account is either $2,000 or $2,500, depending on which brokerage house you'll be using. Since it takes a few days or a week to set up a margin account, it's recommended that you set it up as soon as possible.

The next thing you'll need is *The Slice Trading System.* You need to go to **www.TradeTheSlice.com** to get the complete system. You can't very well expect to master the secret behind trading the markets if you don't have all of the training you need or if you think you'll troll online all day to find a free blog to help you how to do this. I hope that's not what you're thinking. Because if you are – and if you don't believe that you're worth investing in yourself to make sure you do this right by having all of the components and by studying all of the components – then you're just not cut out for this. Only losers think everything should be for free or think that everything should be given to them on a silver platter without them making an attempt to get off the couch. I hope that doesn't describe you otherwise you'll probably never be successful doing anything.

Successful people invest in themselves. They invest in their education. The invest in the time it takes to master something. They invest in their future in that way. Years ago, I was probably like you and most of the people out there – I thought the world owed me something and that if something was truly worthwhile, it should be given to me for free. Then, after I gave myself a little pep talk and make the commitment to this, I look back and think: GOD NO! Nobody should be given this or anything that can really make you thinks kind of money for free! Never! The people who are the deadbeats who would never invest in their future this way should <u>never</u> be able to access to these secrets! So, hopefully you're not one of those deadbeats who thinks all the secrets of the world should be given to you because that's NOT how rich people think at all. That's what I've come to find out in this personal millionaire journey of mine.

The very moment I found out about *The Slice*, I dropped everything to be part of it because there was something inside of me that *knew* it was what I had been looking for. I just <u>knew</u> that this is what I was looking for to become a master millionaire trader. And my gut was right. But the key is here that I DID NOT hesitate. I didn't falter or waffle around or start making excuses about how expensive it was or how there was a learning curve and that I had to go through all of the materials – taking time away from my family – to learn how to do this right. To master this. NONE of that went through my head because I realized very early on how important it was for me to learn how to do this right and to be able to make loads of money doing this.

I was really lucky to be part of a small handful of people who did a one-time-only workshop with Dr. Peter Barrington himself. This was right before he got really sick. I was in a small room with only a dozen trading student and I just knew that I was part of something special. And it turned out to be very special because after that one event he hasn't done another one since. He hasn't been well enough to continue that workshop legacy.

I consider myself very fortunate and very lucky to have learned this stuff first-hand from Dr. Peter Barrington himself. And now you're learning exactly what I learned first-hand.

Back to *The Slice*, consider this your education to learn how to potentially make an incredible cash flow from trading ETFs. It never ceases to amaze me how people are willing to throw hundreds of thousands of dollars away on a "traditional" education by going off to an Ivy League university (or any college, really) just to barely make end's meet after they graduate yet people will balk at spending a thousand bucks or so on an education like this.

I remember being at UCLA and, even back then, each time my tuition bill was due, I could feel my stomach turn into knots because I'd have to cough up *tens of thousands of dollars* each crack. Yes, it was a lot of money (which is why eventually I dropped out of college). Yet I've talked to people who, if they can't get this kind of life-changing information off a free blog or from a $10 book on Amazon, they start bitching and complaining that it must be a "scam" or something.

If anything is a scam, it's the school system that you were brainwashed into believing it could help you create a life-long dream of financial freedom by earning a piece of parchment paper that you hang on your wall in your home office. If anything is a "scam," paying over $100,000 for that piece of paper and for the "honor" of having a decade or more of student debt to pay is the biggest sham of all! And yet too many people are so stupid, they don't see it that way at all.

Once you have been indoctrinate into the world of *The Slice* with Dr. Peter Barrington, you get to communicate with him directly! How powerful is that?!

Even better, if you feel that you need to trade alongside of someone until you get the hang of all of these markets and the way these geometric angles lay down on the charts, I highly recommend the monthly Hot Tips Membership. There's more information about it on the website: TradeTheSlice.com under the Membership link. But…you have to get The Slice System first before you'll be allowed to have the Hot Tips Membership. I have a membership, even though I'm highly proficient in charting *The Slice* and all of these patterns out. I keep the membership as kind of a security blanket to help me validate that I'm doing all of this right. Dr. Barrington still does the picks and newsletter himself so it's probably as close to him as you'll get until he gets better.

When you get *The Slice Trading System*, give yourself time to learn it. It does take a little bit to get the hang of it but, stick with it because I know you'll get it. It took me time to get it and, the key is, I never gave up. I stuck with it. I got into the Hot Tips Membership and traded alongside of Dr. Barrington himself. And I even emailed him if I got stuck and he always got back to me right away to explain things a little better. So, you have that option to just by owning *The Slice System*. You can email Dr. Barrington directly.

As a legal side-note, you cannot ask him to personally forecast the market for you. I tried this one time and got a lashing for it. He's not legally allowed to do that. But if there is a charting question you're stuck on or something that you don't understand *after* you've gone through all of the course materials, he can help you out. He just gets mad when people bother him and they haven't gone through the course and he can tell right away if you haven't. He gets really mad when people do that to him so go through the course a few times FIRST before sending him an email. He's definitely a bridge you DO NOT want to burn and you will if you bother him all day with stupid questions that are answered in the course itself. He'll blacklist you from his email account so you don't want that to happen. After all, when will there every be any other time that you can get advice directly from a master like him? Probably never again in your lifetime. Don't ruin this opportunity to work directly with him by acting foolish.

Well, my time with you has come to an end. I've really enjoyed being able to teach you what I know and what I've learned since becoming a trader and I really hope you carry on and become successful in the markets.

This is a really exciting time for you. Think about it. If you knew that you had the potential of making a million or more per year in profits – and by never leaving your house – then it is highly recommended that you learn every aspect and component to this secret trading method like the back of your hand. If you don't or if you're too lazy to learn then you're not going to make the kind of money that you want. However, if you really do want to master this, I recommend going through all of your course components over and over again until this becomes second nature. Make sure you paper trade before trading real money in the markets. And make sure you feel comfortable paper trading before you even attempt to trade real money. Anyway, take it easy. Have a good time trading. And never be afraid of the process. Learn this stuff well, trade with confidence, and make a lot of money in the process.

Your friend,
*Robert Savoy*

## LAST CHANCE to Get Your Free Jesse Livermore Action Checklist Poster and Free Audio Seminar!!

**Discover How You Can Grab the Highly-Coveted Rules of Trading Checklist You'll Refer to Again and Again Throughout Your Profitable Trading Journey...For FREE!**

**To Discover How You Can Obtain These POWERFUL TRADING RESOURCES That You'll Be Using to Direct Your Most Profitable Trades FOR FREE...
Call Our 24-Hour HOTLINE Now at:**

# 1-800-990-0028

www.SevenFigureTrading.com

Former Secret Society Member Reveals Shocking Admission...

# "Donald Trump is Right! The System is Rigged Against Every 'Average American.' And Even Worse, It's Carefully Designed to NEVER Allow Most to Ever Gain Any Wealth Unless You Know of This One SIMPLE SECRET!"

**How a Former Skull and Bones Secret Society Member – Who Wants to Be Referred to As "Mr. X" – Cracks Open the Plans of New World Order and Reveals Some DISTURBING NEWS About What is in Store for the Common Man and Woman of America in Years to Come. What They Have Planned is SHOCKING As Their Plan Continues to Unfold to Include Stripping Everyone of Their Privacy, Freedom, and Ability to Acquire ANY Power and Wealth.**

## This Will Be the Most Important SECRET You Ever Read...*It'll Save Your Life!*

Dear Friend,

*This could be the most important book you ever read.* In fact, your life could depend on what lies in your hands right at this moment.

You see, many years ago the Secret Societies of the world decided – *with precise calculation and accuracy* – how the masses of the population would be <u>controlled</u>. And what is about to happen next in our economy will be nothing short of earth-shaking and shocking to you.

**Reality Is...You Are <u>NEVER</u> Meant to Become Wealthy or to Gain <u>ANY</u> Power. And You Never Will Be Either So Long As You Stay in the Dark About What's *Really* Going On!**

Rockefeller created the school system with the *sole intent* of training (brainwashing) the masses to become *subservient* to the wealthy, powerful and elite. This system began "programming" what the heads of the Secret Society would refer to as "the herd" (as in cattle).

The herd was "molded" to become passive, dependent, and reliant on the elite for their every need including a job to support their households. This was an intended form of *active* brainwashing, creating nothing more than a mass population of people who were discouraged from thinking for themselves.

Then something got out of control. A few of the herd got crafty, creative, and opportunistic. They were able to take advantage of profit opportunities before the elite had the chance to adapt and fully understand this new technology that quickly swept the world: the Internet. **There was only one thing for them to do:**

## The Elite Had to Choose to Let *Some* Newcomers Into Their Secret Societies Who Would Play Their Game While Destroying Those Who Didn't Play By Their Rules

If the elite were unable to control a newly wealthy and powerful, their power would become old hat. They had to find a way to control those who were able to use the technology of software development and the Internet to rapidly gain wealth. No one outside of the Society was allowed to have enough power and wealth to control things in a new way…*their way*.

And Society Members had to find a way to nip this in the bud.

To do this, they would either add these new members, making them part of the Secret Society, giving them a limited role and a false sense of power. Or they would find ways to destroy those who did gain massive power and wealth through appropriate legal channels, beating them relentlessly in commerce, or by eliminating them altogether through ending their life.

Usually a good solid threat of death was good enough for most to keep them in line.

It didn't work for Jimmy Hoffa or many others who gained wealth and power too fast.

It didn't work for John F. Kennedy either. Next will be Donald Trump.

People who rock the boat get *eliminated*. And fast! That's just how the game with the elite works.

But with the power of the Secret Society having limitations due to today's fast-moving technology, allowing almost any Tom, Dick, or Harry the opportunity for vast power and wealth, the elite has had to create a new strategy to control the masses. This would be done through something called the Newest World Order.

## **The Plan to Put 85% to 90% of the American Into Poverty is Happening in Full Force RIGHT NOW!**

*You are in trouble.* If you represent the middle class on ANY level – whether you are lower-middle, middle, or upper-middle class – you are in *jeopardy* of being shoved down into the lower 85% to 90% income bracket that will represent what the elite has already coined as the "New Poor."

Slowly but surely, without notice by most people, inflation is creeping up while wages haven't increased much over the past two decades. Work opportunities are vanishing as robots and automation systems take over. Pretty soon A.I. (Artificial Intelligence) will be doing most jobs that Americans are doing now. If you thought companies going overseas was bad, it'll be worse when A.I. takes over. There is no job security. There never really was in the first place.

The idea of the elite is to keep the average American spinning their wheels, looking for the next buck while being immersed in their iPhones, playing video games or watching TV, never looking up to see what's *really going on* before their very eyes. But…what *is* really going on? What *is* happening to us? The better question is: What *are* they doing to us?

## The Elite Are Looking for Powerless Slaves…But They *Only* Need a Handful of Us! The Rest Will Have to Be "Disposed" Of…*Including <u>YOU</u> <u>TOO</u>!*

With robots, automation and A.I. taking over, the elite will soon fully exhaust their use for us. Too many people milling around is too hard to control. Those that the elite have no use for will have to be disposed of. *Soon.*

You'll notice that in many less desirable areas of the country, there will be strange diseases, extremely poor food and meat quality, exposures to toxins (as with the water in Flint, for example), and sudden unexplainable deaths ruled as untimely yet "natural."

You'll find that, as time goes on, more and more of these kinds of deaths will take place. Hardly anybody will notice. There will be no articles or television air time devoted to such stories. After all, it is happening to those in poor areas. And the elite control all of the media outlets anyway. Therefore, none of this will ever be reported for most to take notice. This is already happening at an alarming rate!

As more and more people are pushed down into the lower 85% to 90% (since the middle class will cease to exist altogether in a few more years), more and more of these untimely deaths will continue to occur yet they will go unnoticed by those who matter: the rich and elite. If you're not concerned about being poisoned by the beef you buy at your local grocery store, worrying about heavy metals contaminating your drinking water, or if the next flu shot will do you in...likely these will be concerns you'll have in only a handful of years to come as they aim to take out even more people in our overpopulated society.

## To Avoid Being Categorized and Abused As the 85% to 90% "New Poor," You <u>MUST</u> Become Rich YOU HAVE NO CHOICE!!

You've probably always wanted to be rich anyway, right? Now you MUST become rich if you don't want to be part of the 85% to 90% low class in *abject poverty*. You'll want to be rich for several reasons:

1) To live anywhere you want, ideally *outside* of the United States at some point.
2) To be able to get away from dense suburban areas where water and food supplies are targeted.
3) To be able to afford the highest quality food and medical services.

4) To be able to live how you want without interference or unwanted scrutiny.
5) To be able to live without succumbing to the whims of the elite.

Do you want a piece of that ultra-rich lifestyle, not only to be able to retain your health and happiness but to be able to have the FREEDOMS you deserve to have?

## If You Want to Be Rich, You <u>MUST</u> Become the Millionaire Next Door and Make Money a <u>Certain</u> <u>Way</u>…

What if I told you that there IS a way for you to become as wealthy as you want to be using the oldest systems for attaining wealth (originally developed by the elite) that YOU TOO can use to become wealthy too?

Yes, you can use THEIR OWN SYSTEM of attaining and retaining their wealth to use for creating your own pot of gold. And you can use this system as many times as you want, over and over again, until you make the amount of money you set out to make.

Just don't make too much money. You DO NOT want to get on their radar otherwise they could destroy your life. This means keeping this to a MINIMUM…say about $100,000 per month. You could even ratchet this up to $1,000,000 per month in profits and still fly under the radar. But…beyond that, you'll attract too much attention to yourself.

Do you think you can do this to make anywhere from a handful of Benjamins to keeping a cap on it at $1,000,000 per month? If so, then I have something EXTRAORDINARY to share with you from a very close friend of mine: Peter Barrington. There is ONLY ONE WAY to become wealthy in today's day and age. <u>TRUST</u> me on this one.

*And here it is…*

Mr. X

← This will blow your mind!!

# Check Out *The Slice* Video RIGHT Now!

# www.TheSliceVideo.com

**Ready to Get Started with The Slice? Give Us a Call at (661) 295-5050 Ext. 2 and Talk to a Trading Expert Who Can Better Help You Understand How The Slice Can Potentially Change Your Financial Future!**

**WHY WALL STREET *HATES* THIS <u>ONE</u> <u>MAN</u>...AND WHY <u>YOU</u> WILL WANT TO KNOW <u>EVERYTHING</u> HE KNOWS!**

<u>**WARNING**</u>**: THE STOCK MARKET IS ON THE VERGE OF A TOTAL COLLAPSE AND IF YOU DON'T READ THIS REPORT, YOU COULD LOSE EVERYTHING YOU HAVE! AND EVEN IF YOU DON'T HAVE MONEY IN THE MARKET NOW, YOU CAN STILL LOSE – YOUR JOB (OR YOUR BUSINESS) AND YOUR FUTURE ARE AT RISK – BECAUSE THE ECONOMY IS ABOUT TO TAKE A MAJOR NOSEDIVE. YOU CAN EITHER LOSE EVERYTHING OR GET RICH BEYOND YOUR WILDEST DREAMS! IT'S YOUR CHOICE. THE "WALL STREET MAVERICK" CAN SHOW YOU EXACTLY HOW!**

## Secrets of the Wall Street Maverick:

Dr. Peter Barrington is Wall Street's Most DISLIKED Man...And Why You WILL Want to Know Everything He Does About Trading Like an Insider With a Secret He Uses Called "The Slice"

## "How to GET RICH by *(Legally)* Trading Like an 'Insider' With a Secret Method Called *'The Slice'* That is *So Dead-On Accurate*... It Will Blow Your <u>Freaking Mind</u>!"

While the economy starts to slide into another recession, you stand to lose <u>more</u> <u>than</u> <u>you</u> <u>can</u> <u>ever</u> <u>imagine</u>. The

Wall Street "slaughtering" has only just begun. But if you act now you still have a choice: **LOSE EVERYTHING AND TAKE TO THE SOUP LINES OR EARN YOURSELF A PLACE IN THE TOP 5% OF THE RICHEST ELITE. THERE IS <u>NOTHING</u> IN BETWEEN!** Even if you don't think you know enough about investing, you can make a FORTUNE by using a very simple system that ANYBODY can learn quickly. And this is truly the LAST OPPORTUNITY for the Little Guy to get FILTHY RICH! <u>OR</u> this could be your LAST WARNING for what's about to come!

**In a few months from now you will either be laughing all the way to the bank or standing in the welfare line with just the shirt on your back. Why? Because some MAJOR CHANGES are going on right now!**

We all know about the scandals of recent years of how a handful of selfish people made *hundreds of millions of dollars* while tons of people – too many to count – had lost everything they ever worked for in just a few short months.

**But the WALL STREET SLAUGHTER is <u>NOT</u> <u>NEARLY</u> over yet!** In fact, *it's just barely gotten started!*

Do you remember the days of Enron, Global Crossing, Tyco, and WorldCom? Remember how they were the first to scalp the American public during that time? Maybe this will surprise you. Then again, maybe not. But the Wall Street scalping has only gotten more sophisticated these days. It's been going on *discreetly* for many years now…and continues to take place behind closed doors.  It's now WORSE than ever!  *And it's not about to stop either.*

More giants are about to take a tumble and it's going to shake the economy so hard that everything else will begin to topple like dominoes.  *The big lay-offs at GM is just the beginning of what will become a trend from now through the next 2 years!*  **And even billionaire trader Paul Tudor Jones says that this upcoming recession will be our worst ever!**

Where is *your* money going to be?  Think your money is safe in stocks or mutual funds?  Think your job or business is safe?  Think your investments are safe?  **You are FAR from being safe!**

You will have to make a critical decision right now.  Do you "watch and wait" and foolishly hope that we'll skip a recession and risk everything you have?  Or do you *take action and make a fortune* as the economy takes a big fall?

## We Are About to Experience a Market Collapse That's So Devastating…the 1929 Stock Market Crash Will Seem Like a Picnic in a Park on a Sunny Day!

This is going to be a rough one, folks.  ***Worse* than the Depression and the Great Recession combined!**  And as you know, most of the population back in 1929 – especially those who weren't prepared – *lost everything*.  **The ones who lost the most *didn't even own a single stock*.**

**The same thing happened in 2008.  Most everyone was caught with their pants down while**

**jobs, businesses, savings, investments, and retirement funds were wiped out *virtually overnight.***

And yet there were a *select handful* who were pre-warned and properly prepared…and they created fortunes during this market shift that were *so vast* that the proceeds are <u>still</u> paying them huge dividends and pay offs…and will continue to do so even for their kids, grandkids, and great grandkids!

## Big Monster Corporations that We <u>Rely</u> On for Our Energy, Communication, Transportation, Food, Banking, and Household Necessities Are ALL AT RISK of Crashing to the Ground…<u>AGAIN</u>!

*But how can that be?* Certainly large companies that have been around forever have a strong foothold in the economy. Especially after recovering from our most recent post-2008 Great Recession, right? <u>WRONG</u>!

The first thing I have to say to that is…were you under a rock during our most recent financial bashing our economy took starting in 2008 and *for years* afterwards? Remember what happened with all those banks and financial institutions that were "too big to fail" like Lehman Brothers, AIG, Merrill Lynch, Bear Stearns, Countrywide, Washington Mutual, Fannie Mae and Freddie Mac?? And that *short list* was just the tip of the HUGE iceberg! The fact is, there are WAY TOO MANY to list here. And what *most* people don't know (and will never know) is that we were *less than 36 hours* from a *complete* banking and economic collapse back in the fall of 2008, kind of like what happened to Greece.

And guess what? The banks that did survive (thanks to the government bailout program) are now bigger than ever. Now they're REALLY too big to fail. Only 6 banks own *more than half of the assets* of the entire banking industry. With the rolling back of banking regulations, this looks a lot like the *very same pre-2008 deregulatory agenda* that encouraged excessive risk-taking by mortgage lenders and banks.

Plus, due to financial blatant mismanagement, internal corruption, lack of organization, higher production costs, higher distribution and warehousing costs, the disappearance of consumer protection regulations and agencies that are <u>supposed</u> to protect average people from getting screwed over…and then a MAJOR recession to slap us all in the face – *how many companies – large or small – can endure all of that ALL AT ONCE?? If you don't believe me, just take a close look at what happened to chains like Sears, Toys 'R Us, Kmart, RadioShack, Sam's Club…and the recent massive store closures of J.C. Penney, Macy's, Gap, Payless, Foot Locker, Walgreens and many others.* ***All household names!***

**All of the sharpest and richest market forecasters all agree: there is a huge problem with BOTH personal and commercial debt right now. And all of these signs (including the store closures) are linked to COMMERCIAL debt problems! And with personal debt, we're talking about the VERY SAME subprime credit problems just like back in**

**2008 which ALSO affect BIG CORPORATIONS like banks, lenders, and creditors, for example.**

As these giants are tumbling, we will SLAM into a *huge recession*. <u>AGAIN</u>! And when these big boys all fall down, there will be a "ripple effect" that will tear down the smaller and smaller companies that stand next to it. Very few companies will be left standing. *AGAIN!* **Meanwhile, people will be back out of work!** *AND IN DROVES!! AGAIN!*

**But I'll Bet That I'm Not Telling You Anything New…In Fact, I'll Even Bet That You've "Suspected" This Economic Downfall For <u>AT LEAST</u> a Year Now!**

And why is that? Are you *psychic*? ***Or is it just plain obvious!***

Look what we have been seeing for many years now: Political scandal and cover-ups, white-collar fraud up the ass *like never before*, increasing taxes and interest rates but a decrease in quality jobs and salaries, highly respectable businessmen and politicians suddenly turning sour just to turn a few bucks, greedy multi-billionaires who want EVEN MORE MONEY for no good reason other than to make sure others don't have anything at all, and white-collar crime investigative units that are <u>so</u> <u>overworked</u> that they would have to <u>quadruple</u> their current staff in order to combat even <u>one</u> <u>tenth</u> of the white-collar fraud taking place in this country!

*And why?* Because making money the old-fashioned way isn't working anymore thanks mostly to our "New (Post-2008) Economy."

Baby-boomers are unable to locate employment for the same pay as before (if they're lucky enough to find a job at all) and most don't have enough money to comfortably retire. Prices of homes have skyrocketed but the average pay for your average office worker hasn't gone up in *over* 20 years! Between all of these issues including chronic government shut downs and more prolific off-shoring of the workforce, the middle class is being squeezed more than ever!

And it doesn't help that it takes a MINIMUM of $85,000 a year for a couple to *live frugally* here in Southern California and yet the average job pays $32,000 a year which results in the obvious – *financial struggle with no way out.*

This whole world is turning into DOG EAT DOG just to put a simple meal on the table!
***AND IT'S ONLY GETTING WORST BY THE DAY!***

## The Two Classes in Years to Come: *Very* Rich and *Very* Poor!

Financial forecasters have been predicting the separation of the classes *for decades now*. Well, *they were right*. It's now becoming a full-blown reality faster than we ever thought possible! The middle class will cease to exist by the year 2030 and then the other "cusp" classes will follow. The lower-middle class will be bumped out. Then the upper-middle class will disappear. *Completely.*

Leaving just two classes: The very wealthy and the very low class. It will be just like the old sixteenth century where there were the royals and the servants...*and nothing else.*

And if it's not obvious now, it will be made plain-as-day obvious during this newest economic crisis that is rapidly descending upon us. So, what do we do? How to we make sure we end up on the *right side* of the tracks?

## The ONLY Way to Make a Fortune During This Next Economic Downfall is...

- By discovering how to trade the markets *really really well*...
- By having that EDGE that nobody else has by "knowing" things that nobody else knows, *and*...
- ***By trading a specific TYPE of market INSTEAD of what you're probably used to trading.***
  *AND...perhaps the most important...*
- ***Trading this type of "stock" in a certain way that virtually guarantees dead-on accurate market forecasts each and every time!***

## How I Came to Discover This Secret Will SHOCK You!

My grandfather Robert Barrington (AKA "Bobby B.") knew a man named Jesse Livermore. You may or may not have heard the name before. (I'll tell you more about who Jesse is in a minute.) My grandfather and Jesse were pretty close friends. And during the times they spent together, Jesse would share things with my grandfather about how to trade the markets.

But first of all…*who the hell is Jesse Livermore?*

This will actually SHOCK you!

First let me say, for the record, that I thought my grandfather was a *total piece of crap*. He was a womanizer and cheated on my grandmother every chance he got. And for this, I'll never have any man-to-man respect for him.

*But how is this of any relevance to anything?*

Because *this* is how the story of my granddad Bobby B. and Jesse Livermore started their friendship, while scoping out the scene for new

women to have affairs with while hanging out drinking together for the purposes of looking for women. This would be during the 1920s and the 1930s, as they became fast and longtime friends.

While Jesse Livermore *never wrote* about his secret trading method behind how he scored $100 million by shorting the stock market on Black Tuesday (October 29, 1929 stock market crash) that set off the

Great Depression, he <u>DID</u> tell my granddad how he did it, *in precise detail!*

Most people think that Jesse used a trading strategy called *The Shakeout + 3* but that's NOT how he knew that the market was going to crash. After all, if you take a look at this double-bottom pattern, it's designed for an upcoming bull market, <u>NOT</u> a bear market at all.

Plus, as Jesse himself said, *any fool* can recognize the *Shakeout +3* pattern.

Here's how it works: A cup-with-handle buy point *(10 cents above the high of the handle)* or a flat-base buy point *(10 cents above the high of the left side of the base)*. The conventional buy point comes when the stock starts to rally after the second leg down. Then entry is when the stock crosses above the middle peak in between the two down legs. Add 10 cents and there's your buy point.

*The Shakeout + 3* pattern also comes when a stock starts to rally after the second leg has formed. The buy point is derived by adding three points to the

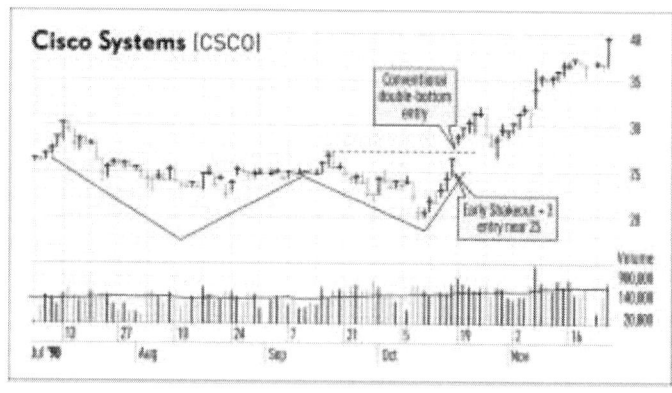

low of the first pullback. So, if the low was 27, add 3 points to get a correct entry at 30. However, the adding of 3 points generally only applies to stocks that are trading in the 20-40 range and requires strong volume when a stock clears the proper buy point.

With higher-priced stocks, it's critical to add more than just 3 points to the first low. It's best to add around 10% of the price of the stock, in this case. If the stock is priced at 60, you can add 5 or 6 points to the low to get the buy point. For stocks that are trading at 100 or more, add 8 to 10 points. This "double-bottom pattern" was in Jesse's book called *How to Trade in Stocks*. It was one of the very rare things he discussed in any of his writings about any "secret trading method" he might have used to when predicting major market moves.

But it's *not really* how he traded, especially when predicting huge market <u>crashes</u> (which is how *big money* is made very quickly). There was actually a completely different way Jesse predicted the market…a way that he NEVER wrote about or revealed *to anyone else* <u>except</u> to my grandfather!

I remember when my grandfather would talk *incessantly* about trading stocks and *The Slice* method that Jesse had shared with him *many times* over the years… which was the *real* trading method he had used for the hundreds of millions of dollars he had made in the stock market. My grandfather even

My Grandfather Robert "Bobby B" Barrington and Me at the Age of 12

drew out illustrations of "The Slice" and showed me how it can work when trading almost anything. But I never cared. I was a young kid. Who would care about stock trading at only 12 years old?

Back then, I'd mow my grandparent's acre-and-a-half of lawn every week. He'd give me a "bonus" by adding an extra 50 cents on top of the regular buck I'd earn from mowing the lawn *if* I could draw *The Slice* on whatever stock chart he chose for that week. Of course I'd do it. I'd earn an extra 50 cents just from drawing a few lines on a piece of paper which took me maybe 25 seconds on my slowest day. He'd always smile, give me 6 quarters, and then walk away with the stock chart I had drawn on. Little did I know what he was *actually trading* with what I had marked on those drawn-on charts until 6 years later when…

# He Showed Me a Margin Account That Had Over $100,000 in It…And Told Me It Was MY MONEY from MY Stock Predictions

**All from a Starting Margin Account of Only $500; And Here Is How It Was Done…With Jesse Livermore's SECRET Trading Strategy Called…**

www.SevenFigureTrading.com

If you've ever had experience with stock, option or bond trading before, these names would probably be familiar to you. They've all written books: Warren Buffett, W.D. Gann, Larry Williams, Ted Warren, Peter Lynch…Yet, why does it seem that no matter how many trading techniques, strategies, and secrets investors waded through most NEVER find the true trader's "secret" to fortunes?

***After all, the key to success in the markets is to know ahead of time what the market will do. That is how REAL traders make a fortune like clockwork.***

***But REAL traders who make REAL money will NEVER give you a secret investing strategy that actually works. Why? Because the bottom line is this:***

> *"The most effective trading system out there!! Slicing the market should be patented because the 'Big Boys' will steal it from you!"* – Edward Coleman, Author of Making Money in the Stock Market

## REAL Traders Know a Trading "Prediction" System That <u>GUARANTEES</u> Successful Trades At Least 90% of the Time But They <u>CANNOT</u> Reveal Their Secrets to You!

They gain *nothing* by telling you their strategies. *Nothing at all!* So, they don't tell you anything! *And they never will!* Why the hell would they? Would <u>YOU</u> tell anyone about a stock secret that can consistently make you $10,000 or more *a minute*? I don't think so! And this is why no REAL multi-million-dollar trader will EVER reveal his or her secrets.

What's even worse is that there are a whole slew of *pretend* "guru" traders will write books, conduct seminars, produce "training" videos and courses…all telling you *nothing more* than the basic fundamentals or market "common sense." And the whole time they are using a system so precise, it makes them look like a trading celebrity because somehow their "system" only works for them. And being that they've written books on their "secret," obviously the rest of us must be stupid for not being able to trade like they do. Meanwhile they get media attention and all the celebrity hoopla of "knowing" something the rest of us don't when they really know nothing at all.

I'm here to tell you that it's all a scam! And that's why you'll never catch me writing a book about trading. I don't want to be associated with the "pretenders" when I know I'm the real thing. So, I'd rather just leave it at that.

By the way, if you've never read one single book on trading in the stock market, you're probably much better off!

W.D. Gann, a trading "genius," claimed to know the secret. He tried to share his trading methods with us in his books but nobody seemed to fully understand his geometric lines and predictions. Why? Because those geometric lines WERE NOT REALLY HOW HE PREDICTED THE MARKET.

Unfortunately, he lived during a time were the world wasn't so open-minded. It was a clear case of Nostradamus-ism where Gann talked in "code" because the close-minded freaks of the early 20th Century may very well have burned him at the stake! (It turned out later on that he didn't do as well as most people thought he did in the market and that Gann, too, was also a "pretender" just to sell stock trading books, courses, and events. Yes, Gann turned out to be a complete sham!)

But what about the REAL movers and shakers of the stock trading world? The ones who will NEVER write a book or speak at a seminar about their secrets? How do *they* trade the markets?

Now, you're probably asking yourself right about now, "Who are you then and why are you suddenly sharing this trading secret?" Good question and you deserve an answer. *So, here it is:*

## After Having Kept This Secret ALL of My Life, I Want to Share This With You Now Before I Pass Away…*Which Will Be Soon!*

I was diagnosed with throat cancer a little more than a year ago. And while I'm in remission now, I know the reality of how these things work. Reality is, I'm not a young man anymore. Far from it. (You can probably tell from my photo on the first page that I'm not very young anymore but I won't tell you how old I am. I'd rather not.)

Reality is, even if I stay in remission for years to come, I know my time will be up sooner than later. And I'm prepared to pass away at any time now.

I woke up startled, realizing something that jump started my heart one morning: *"Nobody else knows this trading secret that I know of! Jesse taught* *my grandfather. My grandfather taught me and a few other family members who ended up <u>never</u> using this powerful trading method because they didn't 'like' trading. So…I'm the ONLY ONE ALIVE who knows how to use Jesse Livermore's most powerful trading secret – the one he NEVER wrote about or taught anyone else <u>EXCEPT</u> for my grandfather."*

And if you're not sure just what a powerful trader Jesse Livermore was, *just look him up*. You'll quickly see just how profitable and on-point he was with ALL of his trades until his personal life ended up in the crapper due to multiple affairs, drinking, and the breakdown of his marriages which was way too much for him to take mentally and emotionally. (This is why he took his own life in the end.)

Just like any other reputable trader, he never shared his secrets with anybody else. Nobody else except for Bobby B. (my grandfather) who passed this strategy directly down to me.

But I'll be honest with you. I didn't share this with a single soul except for my wife and my son. My wife didn't care about it. My son became a doctor and never had an interest in trading. So…that leaves me. And me <u>only</u>.

And pretty soon it'll leave you too. Because I'm making sure I'm getting this secret out there before I pass away because my brother and sisters didn't use this secret, because my wife and son never cared to use this secret…and because I'm the only one that I know of who actually uses Jesse Livermore's <u>REAL</u> trading secret to making such incredible dead-on accurate trades in the market, both big and small.

And I'm passing this secret on to you before I die. Which *won't* be long now.

## The Reason It Took Me <u>THIS</u> Long to Bring This Trading Secret to Light is Shocking!

Wall Street has hated me for as long as I can remember. This is much like the sports bookie hating the guy that always makes the right bet and breaks the house. Or the blackjack player who always wins in Vegas because he's probably counting cards.

People who win in a "betting" game all the time are usually not welcome to play anymore.

I remember a time not too many years ago when a few men in black suits paid me a "visit" to my house. I'm not going to tell you who these men were but I will say that the meeting wasn't pleasant. *At all.* And when I told my attorney about this meeting, at first he didn't believe me. He thought I was pulling his leg.

When I finally convinced him that it really happened by showing him the security video of these guys banging on my front door, he said: *"Don't mess with these guys. This is the type of situation where you find yourself getting killed in some kind of 'accident' or you just disappear. I recommend you keep a really low profile. Take a trip somewhere – for about a year – and then just trade small. Can you do that?"*

Before I could answer, he *hung up* on me! After that he refused any of my phone calls and I never heard from my attorney ever again.

I started to think about it: *Why leave for just a year? Why not just live in Costa Rica or some place like that for the rest of my life? I could trade from anywhere!*

Of course, my wife didn't agree with this idea of being an expat in some foreign land. My son had just gotten married and him and his new wife were planning a family. My wife was excited about grandkids and, truth be told, I really didn't want to leave either.

So, I traded small. What did I need more money for anyway? By this time, I had millions parked in several bank accounts and I had everything I wanted. I kept trading just…because I LOVE IT. I'm a trading junkie, but in a SKILLED kind of way. I'm not like some kind of gambling addict who gets a high on winning once in a blue moon on a game of chance. **MY GAME REQUIRES <u>SKILL</u>.** And to get to my level, you MUST HAVE a "magic bullet secret" of sorts to be as dead-on accurate as I have been with *all* of the trades I've done over the decades.

Since I'm dying now, I don't give a damn about men in black suits or potentially disappearing into the night like Jimmy Hoffa or like the many others who have gained too much power in too little time just by knowing too many secrets. When you get to the point where you know that the game of life is almost over, you become *fearless*. Nothing scares you anymore. Because there's nothing left to lose.

At least that's where I'm at right now. I'm willing to take huge risks to get this secret out there to whoever wants to devote their time in learning this, practicing it, and trading with it to potentially make lots of money for themselves so that I can rest in peace knowing I'm NOT taking this secret to my grave like Jesse Livermore tried to do.

Since I'm the last one qualified (due to the many huge successes I've had in the markets by using this secret) to share this with you, you'd be a complete idiot to NOT want to know what this is. *Because…*

> *"I converted a $150 option into $2,100 in about 2 ½ weeks."* – *Sarah Lynn Gingham, California*

## It All Comes Down to WHAT You Trade and Trading ONLY *This* Kind of Market Can Make You a Fortune

There are MANY different markets to choose from. But I recommend trading alongside of the ***stock indices*** ONLY, hands down. *For me, these markets are much easier to predict!* And, at any given time, usually one is *profiting on a massive scale, long or short*. The stock indices, if you aren't familiar, are the S&P 500, NASDAQ, The Dow (DJIA), and the Russell 2000 among others.

But what I trade are the ETFs that run alongside these markets which is how I make my money since I don't like trading futures. (I started trading commodity futures contracts but, once the ETF versions came into the picture, I started making much more money with minimized risk. So, I left my futures trading activities in the dust since futures can be much too erratic and volatile.) The ETF versions of these markets, for me, are much easier to predict with my *very pinpointed* and specific market forecasting secret: **THE SLICE**.

With these powerful markets, there <u>HAS</u> to be a value based on a multitude of large companies in this "basket" of companies called an "index." These indices moves to the very simple concept of "supply and demand" as a "group" instead of as a singular stock or market. What makes these markets "better" to trade is that there is a mixed value rather than the *emotional value* like in the majority of the stock market. This is why, for the most part, the indices will generally beat almost any other market on any given day because the indices <u>ARE</u> the market (as a whole).

So, how does one trade these markets successfully? Part of my success in this market is *hedging* my trades with options. That's a small part of my trading process and I do this when I'm trading some pretty ballsy market moves.

The big difference between trading "stocks" and "options" is that options tend to be a *much lower risk*. This is why they can be used to hedge against potential market loss on a stock trade or as a method of making money. Or both! And this is why I recommend that if you're just starting out, try trading options only while getting your feet wet.

By the way, an option means that you pay ONLY A FRACTION of the cost of a stock. It's sort of like an insurance policy. If you believe that the market will go up then you will buy your very inexpensive option as "insurance" that you are guaranteed a spot in the market. If the market moves in your favor, you can either exercise the option and secure the stock OR you can <u>sell</u> the option to another trader for A LOT OF MONEY. If the prices of that particular market never move in your favor you only lose the cost of the option which can be as low as $50.

You make money when the market moves in your favor. But how do you know which way the market will move? That, my friend, is the million-dollar question. The question I'm about to give you the answer to…which is:

## What If I Could Show You a Secret Trading Method that Can Make You Fortunes in *Certain Markets* by Using a <u>Single</u> <u>Strategy</u> that Can Dictate Market Moves <u>to</u> <u>the</u> <u>Minute</u>?

As you know, the markets, for the most part, exist on "supply and demand." When there is a shortage, or a "perceived" shortage, then the prices will go up because everybody suddenly wants a piece thinking that they better get it before it's all gone! When there is an overabundance, or a "perceived" overabundance, prices will drop, as everyone will want to get out of the market because it's something that nobody wants, and they better get out before they lose out. When I say "perceived" I mean that most of the time the market moves on the "psychology of the masses." When people "believe" that there is a shortage, they will jump on a stock, even if there really isn't a physical shortage. And if everybody is thinking the same way, it moves the market significantly.

The reason stocks and commodities can be scary is because they move on a *perceived value* of a company stock or commodity. *And that is <u>very</u> dangerous.* There isn't anything to "back up" the stock or commodity except the whim of a bunch of people (traders) who "think" the market may move up or down. As with situations like *Enron* and *WorldCom*, the *perceived value* of a company can be so high on paper, when in reality it isn't worth squat! And in situations like futures contracts – say Soybeans – many times the "value" is based on what a mass group of traders *think* could happen with the supply and demand, not what is *actually happening* with the REAL supply and demand of that commodity.

But let me tell you a little bit about how I use this *groundbreaking trading strategy* that I can guarantee that you've NEVER seen before because NOBODY ELSE but me knows Jesse Livermore's *exact trading method* that can…

## Predict Every Minor and Major Market Move for the REST OF YOUR LIFE

There's a strategy called THE SLICE that you can use to actually "decode" future events of the stock market. Once you learn this one simple method for decoding, you can literally forecast every minor and major market move for the *rest of your life*.

And this is THE secret that Jesse Livermore taught my grandfather who passed it down to me…the one that Jesse *never* wrote about or taught anyone else EXCEPT my grandfather! The one that Jesse planned to take *to his grave*.

Why was my grandfather – Bobby B. – so special to get THE rundown on how this special trading method works? Remember, Bobby B. and Jesse ran together for awhile as the skirt-chasing boozers that they were. And it was during this time that Jesse explained exactly how he traded the markets and was able to predict – *with great accuracy* – every market crash in years before.

> *"This works and I still can't believe it! Thank you for teaching me what I needed to know about trading. Your slice system helped me make $9,000 on the QQQ in just 6 weeks."*
> *– Barney Levine, Texas*

Unfortunately, Jesse's personal life unraveled with unsuccessful marriages, boozing, and a revolving door of women that he lost most of his money. He killed himself in New York in 1940 in the coat closet of a hotel.

What I find most interesting about Jesse is that his method of trading worked like a charm – and it worked EVERY TIME he put it to use with a straight head about him – but he let his personal life get the best of him. He let women and drinking completely derail his personal life and his finances fell apart because he couldn't control his vices.

But with Jesse in my grandfather's rearview mirror of life, he went on to trade himself into a bank account of $45 million. And then, in an interesting twist that I didn't see coming, he ended up giving 100% of that money to charity. I remember when the lawyer – who was the executor of his estate and a family friend – sat me, my brother, my sisters, and my parents in a small office to tell us the news about how we weren't going to inherit a dime. And then he read a note that said something to the effect of:

"**You were all taught how to make money in the markets so you don't need my money. Use what I've taught you all and make your own damned money.**" *What an ass\*\*\*\*!*

So, I did what the bastard told me to do. I put what I was taught *to work* to make my own damned money in the stock market. And I made A LOT of it. In essence, he gave me the greatest gift imaginable: the ability to make my own money whenever I needed it and whenever I wanted it.

## I Started Off Turning $3,000 Into $2.3 Million Dollars in Just 3 Years…All Using Only This ONE Trading Method: <u>THE SLICE</u>

Years ago, I read this one particular stock market book on how this man made two million in the stock market by using these little boxes, which wasn't much different than a geometric pattern called a *narrow, snake-like channel*. I guess he thought he was some kind of genius for figuring something so stupid out on his own.

But really his success all boiled down to LUCK! *Pure dumb luck!*

So many people have come up with "systems" and techniques with cute little names like Japanese candle-sticking, swinging, point-and-figuring, turtling, etc. It sounds awfully good rolling off your tongue at cocktail parties but it's all bull**** when it comes to packing away any money in your margin account. After all, anybody can "backwards" forecast the market (in other words, "forecast" the market <u>after</u> it's already happened) by neatly drawing their little pattern trick on a chart where the action in the market had already occurred.

Nice try. But anybody with a few brain cells in their head can figure out that any scammer can "forecast" a market *backwards* in time using ANY random "method" of their liking and they can convincingly make their little trick "fit" just about ANY chart for just about ANY market.

Since I not only learned this secret of how to REALLY predict the markets and then put it to use on my own, those theories and success-justifications are so funny that it's material for a comedy club…*almost.* It would be funny IF all the *junk bag of tricks* these scammers sold to people didn't make people lose their asses in the market. But they do. Traders just like you can lose A LOT by following some phony primrose path of lies. And that's not funny <u>AT ALL</u>!

**HERE'S A REALITY OF TRADING: YOU CAN NEVER "PREDICT" THE MARKET WITHOUT USING THE SLICE. PERIOD! AND ALL OF THE MOST SUCCESSFUL TRADERS USE THIS METHOD WHETHER THEY REALIZE IT OR NOT!**

Maybe you're starting to understand *how sensitive* this material really is and why the REAL market gurus never said anything about this stuff. It's because knowing this can get people in trouble. It's equivalent to "counting cards" in a casino. Yes, it's legal (because it's a skill used by a brilliant mind) but nobody wants you to use it. So, to stay safe, use this powerful trading secret to trade *small* (a max of $100,000 per month) as to <u>not</u> attract attention to yourself.

So, now is the time to ask yourself…Do you mind using a system that's *unorthodox* yet <u>*powerfully effective*</u> to make yourself millions of dollars in the market in the next few years? Or would you rather stick to candlesticks and people's last names because they impress people at cocktail parties? It's up to you. I don't care either way. Your decision won't change my life in the least little bit.

## "The Slice" That is Responsible for Making My Fortune (and Yours Too in the Weeks to Come)…*But What <u>IS</u> "The Slice" <u>Exactly</u>??*

The wealthiest and most successful top tier traders use one secret: *geometric patterning.* Sound complicated? Don't worry. I didn't do well in high school math either. Yet this is really easy stuff once you learn it. And, the easiest way to predict the market ISN'T by using math or hard-core geometry…but even an easier way. It's because you'll be using only ONE pattern called THE SLICE instead *of the many complicated ones you may have already seen.* All you do is *copy* THE SLICE pattern onto certain charts and you'll be able to forecast the market. This works for both day trading and longer term trades; it works for both just as effectively.

Everything is predicted by *very precise geometric movements* that can forecast where the markets are going

> *"In 4 months my account went from $2,500 to $47,200. You can't argue with results like those, can you?"* – **Robert Barclay, Michigan**

based on what the markets have already done so far. Some of the richest traders discovered that the easiest way to foresee market activity is to see what certain geometric pattern symbols are doing. There are more complicated algebraic and mathematical ways of predicting the market and, if it makes you feel more "righteous" or "smart" to use these methods, you can. Unfortunately, it takes a very long time to master them and many times they don't work for most markets.

By using a symbolic "decoding" method – specifically **THE SLICE** – it's very easy to see which markets will move on which dates. *Yes, you will have the exact dates that these market activities will take place which means that you will know the exact day and time when a market will move up or down!*

*Do you know <u>anyone</u> (other than me) who trades the market who is willing to show you how to "decode" market with that kind of pinpointed accuracy? And what does all this mean for you? TONS OF MONEY!! That's what it means!*

So, how exactly do you "decode" the market?

Okay, let's not get ahead of ourselves. First, let me talk about the types of markets I trade using THE SLICE. I trade ONLY alongside the stock indices. I don't mess around with anything else. And I make an absolute fortune with these markets. I don't waste my time using THE SLICE with any other type of market because – well, truth be told – THE SLICE is only designed with *dead-on accuracy* to work with the indices only. When trying to apply THE SLICE to other markets, you'll find yourself struggling to make it work. So take my word for it and don't bother! There are hundreds of millions of dollars to be made with these specific indices so that should be good enough for you.

So now you're probably wondering, what does THE SLICE look like and how do you use it?

## I'll Show You <u>EXACTLY</u> How THE SLICE Works in "The Slice Trading System" Because I MUST Explain It to You in Full, Precise and Accurate Step-by-Step Detail

There's NO WAY I can accurately describe to you the simple step-by-step strategy in what THE SLICE is and how to trade it with dead-on accuracy within this short report because there are many elements I MUST explain to you first if you are to become a market wiz with this trading secret.

What I can show you now is *an overview* of how to work with this highly effective little-known trading strategy:

1. Looking over current charts and pricing information for one of the stock indices; one of my favorites to trade is the SPDR S&P 500 (SPY) so I suggest you start there if you're not sure where to start.

2. Then you'll simply "map out" THE SLICE by applying this symbol to the current chart in a certain way.
3. You'll then place your trade, ideally online with a place like *eTrade.com*. (You'll need a minimum of $2,000 to start your margin account with them.)
4. Wait until the market moves in your favor, having "protections" in place for safety.
5. Wash, rinse, and repeat…*many times over <u>as fast</u> <u>as</u> <u>you possibly</u> <u>can</u>!*

If you can look at a symbol and apply it to a chart…then you can "decode" stock index ETFs. It's that simple. I do it. And you can do it too. But you must know what this *geometrical pattern symbol* is, which charts to apply it to, which position to use for this symbol (because you can use it in multiple "positions" and sizes), and for exactly which markets use THE SLICE on to make the most money in profits as possible.

The only way I can really show you how to do this is through my "workshop-style" teaching technique. This is how my grandfather taught me how to do it – although he did these exercises verbally with me – and I'll be teaching you how to trade the way Jesse Livermore did it by having you learn each step the exact way I learned it…except in a workbook format. You will shown every detail about how to work THE SLICE in the easiest learning method possible!

Yes, I'm going to teach you how to trade your way to a fortune by giving you an at-home "workshop." No, you won't have to wade through a bunch of CDs, videos, and manuals to figure this out. I have the entire course laid out *workshop style*. It's going to be equivalent to me personally being by your side, showing you how to *decode* the market using *The Slice*, how to paper trade (to get some practice in before doing the real thing), how to execute orders, and how to make money by giving you "hands on" instruction which is the *fastest way* to learn! *You'll be a trading pro in a week!*

Now, I'm not going to insult your intelligence by mapping out a bunch of past market activity to try to demonstrate how great I really am as a trader. Anybody can do that because PAST IS PAST. It's already over. So a chart full of drawings from the past several years mapping out how and where I made all my money, isn't going to help. *What I would like to do is tell you about the future*…

## One Market is About to **COMPLETELY CRASH** and, If You Don't Know Which One It Is…You'll Miss Out on a *Once in a Decade* Multi-Million-Dollar Opportunity!

Instead of concentrating on PAST market moves, I'm going to tell you about stuff that's about to happen VERY SOON. As in, what's about to happen IN THE NEXT 60 DAYS!

Within the next couple of months, there are *three different trading opportunities* that can make you *extremely rich*. One in particular is about to completely drop after having been a little stagnant for several months. And because it's been relatively stagnant, the cost to trade the stock option will be less than $100 each option, if you decide to trade options! That means that sinking only a few hundred dollars will be responsible for a *huge fortune*.

Yes, you can *and should* start out trading OPTIONS instead of trading the actual index fund ETFs

themselves as an extra layer of "safety" if you're not quite ready to go "all in" just yet.

But you have to know which stock index ETFs are going to drop and <u>when</u> they're going to

| Stock Index ETF #1 | Stock Index ETF #2 | Stock Index ETF #3 | Stock Index ETF #4 | Stock Index ETF #5 |
|---|---|---|---|---|
| Call – 3 weeks | Call – 7 days | Call – 5 weeks | Put – 3 days | Call – 2 weeks |
| $7,800 | $2,400 | $6,500 | $1,100 | $4,900 |
| Put – 2 weeks | Put – 10 days | Put – 1 week | Call – 10 days | Put – 5 days |
| $4,700 | $3,300 | $2,000 | $2,300 | $1,800 |

move…otherwise you can't cash in on this upcoming opportunity!

Check out these actual *decoded predictions using THE SLICE* that are going to happen in the next few weeks…

| Total Amount Possible Within 6 Weeks | $36,800 |
|---|---|

"Call" indicates trading an option in a market when you are predicting that prices going up. "Put" indicates trading an option in a market when your position is to take profits when the market drops. You can make money on BOTH the incline and decline of the market which I'll show you how. Actual dollar amounts in the chart are based on *close estimations of what you can make in the upcoming weeks ahead*. These actual stock index ETFs are, according to my geometric symbol decoding calculations, due to make these jumps in the next several weeks.

Now, sometimes $36,800 is "usual" in 6 weeks, sometimes it's not a lot at all. Sometimes it's mere peanuts. For example, with the recent drops in the NASDAQ and S&P 500, some people made *several hundred thousand dollars* in just a few weeks! Some made this in just a few days! Some people MADE MILLIONS during these same time periods! In the chart above, I'm simply giving you a demonstration of what my predictions are for the upcoming weeks.

*"I was able to profit $9,450 my first month. My second month was a bit better at $11,300. I'm 53 years old. How come I didn't learn about this much earlier?"* – Teddy O'Reilly, Washington

As I said, one of the most lucrative markets about to make a MAJOR DROP within the next few weeks. This drop alone can be worth *a million or more* to you depending on *how you play the market*. Yes, one million dollars or more IF you play it right! And I will reveal this *exact* market to you, exactly what date you need to get in the market, and exactly how to play the market so you can make the most money possible when you invest in *The Slice Trading System*.

Yes, you better get on this ASAP otherwise you will probably miss out making these kinds of profitable trades if you end up dragging your feet, taking forever to make a decision on whether you want to do this or not, or if you get the materials and let it sit on your desk for awhile. In which case, you probably won't end up profiting at all.

So, it you're one of these lazy, indifferent, on-the-fence or skeptical people then don't bother learning how to do this. I didn't decide to risk it all to get this secret out there just for it to land on some lazy jerk's desk who will "get around" to going through the stuff..._someday_. If that describes you, skip this opportunity. This is only for those who are raring and ready to start ripping through this stuff the hot second the box ends up at their doorstep!

One more thing: I have a CD that you'll be getting when you invest in The Slice Trading System in the next 24 hours that has all the stock index ETF charts on it and it includes THE SLICE laid down on these charts, showing you where the market is about to go next! You DO NOT want to miss out on getting this free CD so you MUST hurry and get this system RIGHT NOW before this offer goes away!

## Aren't You TIRED of Taking 2 Steps Ahead and 3 Steps Back in the Market?
## Aren't You Just TIRED of <u>LOSING</u> Yet??

A lot of traders I've met over the years have this one thing in common: they make some gains, think they've finally nailed "the secret" of trading the markets, and then they lose it all quickly thereafter..._plus_ _some_.

And on and on this madness goes. *Where it stops, nobody knows!*

When are you going to get SICK of being on the losing end of the trade? After all, when YOU LOSE, people like me pick up your losses as OUR GAINS. Aren't you just tired of playing that game? Aren't you tired of being on the *losing side* most of the time?

Trading the markets was never a game that was meant for you to win. Just like gambling in Vegas, the entire system is stacked in such a way that the Average John Q. Trader will <u>NEVER WIN</u>.

> *"Absolutely outstanding! The best trading system out there, hands down!!"* – *Andrew C. Scott, Editor of* **The Stock Letter**

And it's only a small handful of traders like me who know how the markets work and how to stack the market to their advantage.

You can now be one of those traders. Instead of being on the losing side of every trade, you can now be on the winning side your trades!

You can still get into the "rich" class by becoming an investor. In fact, investing is the <u>ONLY</u> way left to secure the highest standard of living and to actually become wealthy at these elite levels. Sure, you can own a business…but rather the business WILL OWN YOU INSTEAD, *if it survives the crash of the economy*. So, why go down that path at all??

As Robert T. Kiyosaki, author of *Rich Dad, Poor Dad* indicates in all of his books that the only way to have wealth beyond your wildest dreams is to have a BIG, multi-million or multi-billion dollar business like *Microsoft* <u>OR</u> become an investor. Most of us don't have the millions of dollars or skillset required to start a BIG business nor do we want that kind of stress. So, *that leaves one thing:* INSTING!

Investing is truly the LAST OPPORTUNITY for the Little Guy to get rich. The middle class will soon be eliminated altogether. Which class will you choose? The poor or rich? Right now you CAN choose. *Before it's too late!*

## How to Turn 90% or More of Your Trades Into Potentially Making $20,000+ Monthly With Much Less Risk Than With Your Conventional Risky Trading Instruments

I will not only show you some of the more popular success fundamentals of how to make money in the market but I will also show you my special market "decoding" method called THE SLICE that virtually guarantees that 90% or more of your trades will make you money which can be worth up to $20,000+ per month MINIMUM!

I'm going to show you everything you need to know and, the way I have this course set up is workshop-style, so you can quickly move through the materials, understand everything you are learning, and get yourself making money in the real market as quickly as possible! I'm going to show you how to:

- ✓ Make thousands a month *in pure profits* with LOW RISK
- ✓ Gain maximum market leverage with low-cost options

- ✓ Use *The Slice* "symbol" to make dead-on-accurate market predictions
- ✓ Map out accurate trades in less than 20 minutes a day
- ✓ How to make a steady income year after year
- ✓ And why this is the BEST opportunity out there!

One thing I wanted to mention is this: You can MINIMIZE your risk by trading options instead. (And yes, THE SLICE works both ways since you're actually predicting the *direction* of the market which has no bearing on whether you are trading a stock, future, ETF or an option.)

When you are trading options, you don't risk any more money than what you paid for the option. This is a lot different than trading stocks or futures contracts, which means when the market moves against you, you <u>INSTANTLY</u> lose. In fact, you can also lose whatever money you have in your margin account PLUS any assets you have if the market moves way against you. ***And that's scary!***

With an option, if you pay $50 for it, THAT'S THE MOST YOU CAN LOSE! If you pay $100 for it, that's all you can lose NO MATTER WHAT! Trading stock index ETF options is the SAFEST way (*if* there is such a thing as "safe" when it comes to trading) to go and I highly recommend everyone start out trading this way.

I've seen so many people lose everything they've had in the stock or futures markets. They either didn't know what they were doing or the market took an unexpected turn for the worst.

*But not with options.* It's the *only* way to get a big chunk of the market without risking your home, cars, savings, etc. Plus, you will first be "paper trading," or trading on paper, for a few weeks or until you feel comfortable with putting real money into the market. I will show you, "workshop" style, *exactly* how to paper trade so you can get yourself into the market and making money as quickly as possible.

(Please note that if you choose to trade stock index ETFs and not mitigating your overall risk by trading options, you can. I just don't recommend it, at least in the beginning and until you get a really strong feel for what you are doing.)

## I'm Looking for a Few Good Men and Women to Share My Highly-Coveted Secret Trading Strategy With…*Before I Die!*

**I ONLY want to work with people who are DEAD SERIOUS about wanting to do this.** So, if you're one of those people who order things just to look at the shrink-wrapped system in the box just to send it right back without opening the packaging, DO NOT WASTE MY TIME. If you're like that then you're just a deadbeat and I don't want you to even TOUCH *The Slice Trading System* because you don't deserve to have something of this *powerful magnitude* to begin with.

For those of you who ARE serious about doing this, know this: ALL of the secrets to making money using *The Slice* are included in your system course materials. NOTHING is left out. And if you have questions, you have access to *unlimited* consultation through fax or email with <u>me personally</u>. (My personal email is **pb@peterbarrington.com**.)

Plus, if you still have questions? Ready to get in on The Slice Trading System? **CALL: 661-295-5050** *Monday through Friday between 9am and 5pm Pacific Time.* You can talk to me personally if I'm available or you can talk to one of my knowledgeable associates.

I'm looking forward to taking you under my wing and showing you this amazing trading secret. It's a true game-changer. And it's about to completely BLOW YOUR MIND in ways you've *never imagined* before. Trust me on this one.

Your friend,

Dr. Peter Barrington
*Trading Multi-Millionaire*

P.S. Call if you want in on trading *The Slice* <u>IF</u> there's still availability: **661-295-5050** between Monday and Friday, 9am to 5pm Pacific Time.

**P.P.S. We ONLY want to work with those who are THE MOST SERIOUS students of trading. When you call about The Slice, we're going to be asking your questions to see if you are the right fit for this trading system...*or not*. If you're not, we'll kindly turn you away.**

# Real People Just Like You Who Are Making Money with THE SLICE...

**Larry Pinellas** started with a $2,000 margin account and was able to grow it to $11,260 in less than 60 days trading only the QQQ. He considers himself a very conservative trader. He has this to say about *The Slice*: *"Very impressive! I started out paper trading for 3 months because I wanted to make sure I had this right. I just started trading with real money and I'm just blown away at the accuracy of this thing called 'The Slice.' I can't imagine trading without it. I wouldn't dare!"*

**Chino Gutierrez** considers himself new to the world of trading. He traded futures many years ago and "lost his shirt," as he describes it. Needless to say, he was extremely hesitant in trying to trade again. *"I liked the sense of shouldering less risk with this system which is the only reason why I took the leap to try it. Like you said, this is a game changer in more ways than one. For me, I paper traded for 2 weeks then opened a margin account with $3,500. I doubled this money in 3 weeks then doubled it again in 2 months. No, it's not 'big money' but it's really an encouraging start. I know that I'll keep doing better as I keep doing this!"*

**Jimmy Curtis** is a long-time seasoned trader and fancies himself an expert of sorts in the markets. He thought he's heard of everything when it comes to trading tricks, gimmicks, and techniques…until he came across *The Slice*. *"I felt like I was reborn when I started going through the workbook for The Slice System, like I didn't know a single thing as a trader before that day. I kind of wished that I learned this as a young boy because I feel like I wasted years trading the wrong way. Finally I'm making money and I feel like I can sleep at night without worrying about losing my ass in the market!"*

---

Required Disclaimer: There is a substantial risk of loss trading the stock market with or without this or any other advertised product, service, or system. Past results are not necessarily indicatives of future results. No representation is being made that any account will or is likely to achieve profits or losses similar to those shown. Do not trade with funds you cannot afford to lose.

# ♣ The Top 5 Questions People Ask Me Every Day About THE SLICE TRADING SYSTEM:

### QUESTION 1: Does this really work?

**ANSWER:** *Yes, it does. <u>Very well</u>! It works even better than you could possibly imagine in your wildest dreams. <u>THAT</u> is how great this works. You just have to give it a whirl to find out for yourself just how powerful and profitable this is.*

### ♣ QUESTION 2: I've lost money in commodities, stocks, options, and/or bonds so I'm a little shy about trying something new. How can I get past feeling so down and negative about the markets knowing I've lost so much already?

**ANSWER:** *Trading the markets certainly isn't for everyone and perhaps trading isn't for you either. Since I don't know you personally, I won't know that answer. You are the one who knows if trading is for you. If you believe it is then you need to have a SYSTEM that works consistently and reliably, over and over again like clockwork. The Slice System is mostly for people who really want to be full-time traders at some point in the future. This isn't for tire-kickers or for people who aren't serious about trading in a serious way. This isn't for doubters or nay-sayers. People who respect and understand trading know just how vital it is in having the right system in place. Likely your losses were because you didn't respect trading enough to have the correct workable system in place, in which you* *should NOT have been trading in the first place because losses were inevitable. First, you must have the RIGHT system. Second, you must apply this system to SPECIFIC markets. Third, you MUST PRACTICE trading on paper for as long as you need to feel confident in your abilities to correctly forecast the market. Fourth, you can then put real money (of $2,000 or slightly more) into a trading margin account. Fifth, you can begin trading VERY SMALL with your newly discovered and learned trading tools to see how it works. If you are satisfied with the results then…Sixth, KEEP TRADING but never taking your eye off the ball. Don't get lazy. Don't ever place trades and walk away, letting the market do the work. Don't become complacent. THAT is how to become a successful trader day in and day out. If you are unable or unwilling to do what I've outlined in this answer, trading is definitely not for you. Instead, I suggest moving on to something else to make money.*

### ✱ QUESTION 3: How must does this cost?

**ANSWER:** *It's not that expensive compared to other systems out there, trading software programs or a college education but it's expensive enough to eliminate broke people, and lazy individuals who won't do anything with The Slice Trading System. People who are given things for free see no value in it. If The Slice Trading System was in a free download report, you'd never take it as seriously as it deserves to be taken. And likely you would never use it. So, I we have an INTRODUCTORY OFFER for only those who qualify to have this system. If you can't afford it or balk* *at the price, this isn't for you. Find a $10 book on Amazon and…we wish you luck with how that will work out for you for your trading. But if you're a die-hard who <u>WANTS</u> this secret to make money in stocks day in and day out – knowing that this could be worth <u>millions</u> each year for you – the price tag on this is MERE PEANUTS in comparison to what this is <u>really</u> worth. Somebody who is reading this now (perhaps you) will know right away the value in what you're getting <u>before</u> you even order The Slice Trading System because you've seen the junkie "systems" that are out there. If you don't see the value at this point and you are whining about the price, this is definitely NOT for you. This is only for those who understand that this is the Holy Grail of trading systems like <u>NO OTHER</u> in existence!*

### ♣ QUESTION 4: Is there a money-back guarantee? What's to stop me from getting it, copying it, and returning it then?

**ANSWER:** *Yes, there is. If you are unsatisfied with The Slice System, you may return it for a refund less shipping/handling provided that it is in re-sellable condition meaning that ALL of the original system seals are intact. If the system has been opened, you'll have to provide 60 days worth of paper trading to apply for your refund. We are so confident that this system works that we've found when people do their paper trading for 2 months, they are shocked and amazed at how profitable the system is that they'd never give The Slice for any reason! We have this strict guarantee* *policy in place to, again, dissuade those who are not serious about doing this from not even bothering to get The Slice in the first place. We ONLY want to work with those who really want to become highly profitable traders. Anybody else who doesn't fit that description…please don't bother us by trying to order The Slice because we won't let you get it!*

✦ **QUESTION 5: I noticed that you have a free newsletter when I order The Slice System. After the free trial period, will you begin charging me? If not, how can I continue receiving this newsletter to get your monthly market trend forecasts?**

**ANSWER:** *You will NOT be charged anything after your free trial period of your newsletter. This is an online version of our Hot Tips Membership newsletter. Once your free trial period ends, you will be given the option of continuing to receive this newsletter of forecasts each and every month thereafter to keep getting my highly reliable predictions and market trend forecasts. We will notify you of how to continue your subscription once your free trial period ends to give you the opportunity to continue receiving this incredible newsletter.*

# "Yes, Donald Trump is Right! The System IS Rigged Against Every 'Average American.' And Even Worse, It's Carefully Designed to NEVER Allow Most to Ever Gain Any Wealth UNLESS You Know This ONE WAY OUT!"

My name is Geoffrey Gold and I'm a business accountant who works on Dr. Peter Barrington's taxes each and every year. I'm here to tell you something disturbing: the system IS stacked AGAINST YOU. You were NEVER MEANT to get ahead. You are NEVER MEANT to get rich. You are just a worker bee in the giant cog of the economic system, meant only to be a SLAVE to the system like a hamster on a wheel, always running and struggling while being intentionally distracted with "fake news," social media memes, and other nonsense. Because the powers that be created this set-up to NOT be easier. You are just a SLAVE to the system, NEVER meant to get ahead. Period!

Geoffrey Gold
*Tax Expert & Accountant*
*Beverly Hills, CA*
*(310) 281-7889*

I first met Peter Barrington many years ago when he needed work done on his taxes...to be done the RIGHT way. He heard of me through the grapevine as being a top business accountant in Beverly Hills so he gave me a call. I thought of him as just another new client – until I saw the MONEY he was claiming on his taxes. Because I always make sure that I cross every "t" and dot every "i," I asked him to send me all of his bank statements and then HAD to ask him, "Are you sure you're making all this money from TRADING the markets?" He assured me that trading was the only form of income for him at that time. (He's since broadened out to invest in property and other things but at the time it was 100% stock trading income!)

This is the REAL DEAL...as REAL as it's ever going to get to bring you closer to the life of your dreams of living the true dream of financial freedom. Are you going to take this opportunity? Are you going to turn it down? It's your choice!

*Geoffrey Gold*

## "I Profited $74,262 in 63 Days by Using *The Slice* – And the Best Part is, I've Only Touched the Tip of the Iceberg!"°

**Michael Littleton, Florida**
*Former Auto Mechanic*

## <u>IMPORTANT</u> <u>NOTE</u>: *If I can teach a high-school drop-out auto mechanic who only made $26,000 a year how to turn his meager $2,000 trading account into high-five figures in only two months, imagine what I can show you!*

---

° **Important Legal Notice Required By Law:** This entire report contains numerous testimonials. Testimonials only provide the perspective of individuals who were successful and satisfied about their experience(s). Testimonials are not representative of most people's experience and provide information just about one person's experience(s) only as to that point in time at which the testimonial was made. Although all testimonials are authentic and accurately represent the comments made, statements made in the testimonials have not been verified. People can and do lose money trading stocks and options and many experts believe that most stock traders lose money. Accordingly, the testimonials herein should not be viewed in any manner as mitigating the risk of loss in stock trading. Stock and option trading is not for everyone, as there is a huge risk of financial loss. Please trade at your own risk with money you can afford to lose. **ALWAYS TRADE AT YOUR OWN RISK!**

"I'm loving life! Your trading secret is superb! I made a killing with the S&P. It brought my account up from $2,500 to $43,227 in about 4 ½ months. Right now I'm sitting on some NASDAQ options which are probably going to make me a lot more money than that! I'll definitely be seeing  you at your next live event. I can't wait! I'm already teaching my son how to do this and he's picking it up pretty quick. Now I have something of real value to pass onto him so he will always know how to make a really good living."

Joseph H. (with Son Anthony), Oregon<br>Full-Time Trader

"Thanks for showing me your trading technique and I especially thank you for the consulting sessions I've had with you. Your tips on the Russell 2000 have profited me almost $7,000. One more thing. I used The Slice on only one S&P 500 option and I was able to make $1,400 in just one week!"

Brett D., Colorado<br>Ski Resort Manager

"My name is Josh and I started trading with your system about 3 months ago. I had previous experience trading but I wasn't very successful. I used The Slice for both the Dow and S&P 500 which  has profited me almost $11,000 on two call options in both markets. The funny thing is, I picked up each option for about $90 each. I'm ready to subscribe to your membership service. Please send me info, by e-mail if possible…"

Joshua K., California<br>College Student

"So far I've made over $13,000 from two options that I cashed out on already because they were getting too close to expiration. I have 5 more options that I'm sitting on. Already each one is worth $3,000 more than I paid for them. Your hotline recommendations really have paid off so far. Big time! Thank you!"

Rich L., California
Real Estate Investor

"I really like your trading approach. It's much different than the techniques I've learned before. I'm still paper trading but I've made $6,000 (on paper) so I feel ready for the market. Thanks for providing such an informative course. I've never seen anything like this before. I'm looking forward to trading real money!"

Duane J., Georgia
Special Education Teacher

# Check Out *The Slice* Video RIGHT Now!

# www.TheSliceVideo.com

**Ready to Get Started with The Slice? Give Us a Call at (661) 295-5050 Ext. 2 and Talk to a Trading Expert Who Can Better Help You Understand How The Slice Can Potentially Change Your Financial Future!**

The Slice™ is a registered trademark belonging to Success For Life. The Slice™ is a copyrighted trading strategy. Seven Figure Trading is copyrighted.
Copyright © 2020   All Rights Reserved!

www.SevenFigureTrading.com

**LEGAL DISCLAIMER AS REQUIRED BY LAW: There is a substantial risk of loss trading the stock market with or without this or any other advertised product, service, or system. Past results are not necessarily indicatives of future results. No representation is being made that any account will or is likely to achieve profits or losses similar to those shown.** Except where identified as actual profits, references to profits may reflect profits in hypothetical or simulated trading. Hypothetical or simulated performance results have certain inherent limitations. Unlike an actual performance record, simulated performance results do not represent actual trading. Also, since the trades have not actually been executed, the results may have under- or over-compensated for the impact, if any, of certain market factors, such as lack of liquidity. Hypothetical trading results are also subject to the fact that they are designed with the benefit of hindsight. No representation is being made that any account will or is likely to achieve profits or losses similar to those shown. Be aware that investment in any of these markets including stocks, bonds, options, futures and/or ETFs have large potential rewards, but also large risks. You must be aware of these risks and be willing to accept them to invest in the markets. Do NOT trade with money you can't afford to lose. Your decision to trade any market – whether presented as low risk or high risk – should be based on your particular financial circumstances and trading objectives. You can achieve profits far less or far greater than represented in these materials. There are absolutely no income guarantees. **Always trade at your own risk.**